HEARING THE PARABLES
OF JESUS

Hearing the Parables of Jesus

Pheme Perkins

PAULIST PRESS
New York, N.Y./Ramsey, N.J.

Library of Congress
Catalog Card Number: 80-84508

ISBN: 0-8091-2352-5

Published by Paulist Press
545 Island Road, Ramsey, N.J. 07446

Printed and bound in the
United Sates of America

CONTENTS

Bibliographical Note

The *Revised Standard Version* of the Bible is the English translation used in this book. It will be helpful to have a version which includes the apocrypha, since we do refer to Sirach and Wisdom of Solomon. It is easier to compare the versions of parables in the different gospels, if you use gospel parallels. The most readily available is:

Throckmorton, B.
1965
Gospel Parallels: A Synopsis of the First Three Gospels. New York: Nelson.

The complete Gospel of Thomas may be found in:

Guillaumont, A. *et al.*
1969
Gospel According to Thomas. New York: Harper.

Robinson, J.M. ed.
1977
The Nag Hammadi Library in English. San Francisco: Harper & Row, 118-30.

Other Jewish writings from the time of Jesus can be found in:

Charles, R.H.
1963 (1913)
Apocrypha and Pseudepigrapha of the Old Testament: Pseudepigrapha. London: Oxford. (Assumption of Moses; 1 Enoch; 2 Baruch; IV Ezra; Testaments of the Twelve Patriarchs).

Vermes, G.
1975
The Dead Sea Scrolls in English. Baltimore: Penguin.

INTRODUCTION

The past decade has seen a flourishing of parables study. The historical analysis of the seminal work of Jeremias and Dodd has been supplemented and challenged by methods from various disciplines in the humanities: literary criticism, philosophy, psychology, anthropology. Yet the more innovative and interesting of these studies have spent so much time defending their new approaches that they have analyzed relatively few parables in detail. The average reader has been left wondering how all this fuss might enrich his or her reading of the parables. This book is intended for such readers, though scholars may also find some of its interpretations challenging to the usual run of assumptions. Each chapter will introduce issues in the current discussion of the parables and the teaching of Jesus. It will then focus on the reading of specific parables. These readings do not pretend to be exhaustive. Rather they seek to present the various directions in which the interpretation of a parable might lead. The parable, as we shall see, is a multivoiced challenge to the hearer: "What do you say?" Finally each person has to give his or her own response.

Jesus' Speech for the Kingdom

Scholars influenced by the work of philosopher Martin Heidegger began to ask what world is established by the parables. They began to emphasize the poetic and aesthetic qualities of the

1

parables as a means of presenting the hearer with Jesus' experience of faith in God. His mode of speech is different from that of other teachers. He did not come interpreting provisions of the Law like a scribe or Pharisee. Sometimes, he spoke words of warning like a prophet or used the proverbs of a teacher of wisdom. Yet he also spoke with a striking newness and authority. When challenged to explain or defend his vision of God, Jesus often replied in the metaphors and stories referred to as parables.

Jesus claims that the rule (this word is often translated "kingdom") of God is approaching; this is something that people can grasp. The world in which that rule may be experienced emerges in the images and stories of the parables. They present a picture of humans and their relations with each other. Through these relations, one finds that the religious stance of a person with God is at stake. The parable is not just some rule or philosophical truth. Ricoeur [1974:101f] suggests that we would have to use one of two forms of speech to state the message of a parable. We might employ a proverb, a wise observation about the concrete realities of human life and behavior, or a prophetic statement, an indication of how people stand in relationship to God. As a teacher of wisdom, Jesus calls our attention to details of human life and behavior that we often overlook. As a prophetic preacher, he calls for repentance and recognition that certain arrangements and accommodations that people take for granted must be transformed by the presence of God's rule. Two different approaches to divine presence underlie these two ways of speaking. It is manifest in all the dimensions of a bountiful creation (wisdom). It stands over against the deficiencies of human behavior as judgment and redemption (prophetic). Jesus' parables disclose a religious dimension to common, human experience. They might be described as a poetry that seeks to establish God's rule in our lives.

The Transmission of Jesus' Parables

Jesus' teachings were not recorded. They were passed on by telling and retelling until they were finally put into written collections. The gospel writers seem to have used such collections of Jesus' teaching. We also have another collection from Syria in the second century A.D. called the *Gospel of Thomas* (GTh). It is written in Coptic but some Greek fragments of sayings in that collection have also been found in Egypt. Though GTh itself is later than the gospels and has been presented in accord with the heterodox views of the Gnostic Christians who preserved it, some of its sayings and parables may represent genuine traditions from the first century. Oral transmission of stories characteristically adapts the story to the changing circumstances of the audience. Since the teachings of Jesus belong to such a tradition, we often find different versions of the same story. Sometimes the language of one version is so typical of the evangelist in which it occurs that we can attribute some of the changes to his own preaching.

Some variations are necessary because the original audience of the parable has changed. Jesus spoke to people who were not convinced of the truth of his teaching. Some may have even been openly hostile. Perhaps some members of his audience saw themselves reflected or made fun of in the characters of the parables. Other people in the audience may have been laughing to see a Pharisee or a rich person in a tight spot. Sometimes we can guess from the content of the story what the occasion that provoked it might have been. In other instances, we cannot be sure that we have situated it correctly in the ministry of Jesus. Christians, on the other hand, preserved the stories as guidelines for their own behavior. They are not an audience of skeptics looking to be persuaded. They see the parables as guidelines for their own attempts to live out Jesus' vision. They also see them as explanations for some of the things that happened to Jesus—particularly, his rejection by others and even the deliberate action against him taken by Jewish authorities. The evangelists preserve the parables for such a Christian audience. They often set them in a context that highlights those points which were important for Christians in their communities. Thus you can see that any parable has several audiences. We can ask about the audience that might have been listening to Jesus. That audience itself is diverse. It includes curious onlookers, the skeptical, religious authorities, those who were hoping to be persuaded, and finally, Jesus' own disciples. Each group might react quite differently to a story. Then there are the Christian audiences of the evangelists. What does a parable say to them about following Jesus? About Jesus' fate and their own?

Approaches to a Parable

Our brief discussion of parables suggests that several approaches are required. We want to ask historical questions. What is behind the parable? How does it fit into the teaching of Jesus and later into the teaching of the early Church? We have to ask literary questions. How are the versions related? How is the story put together as a literary creation? Where does it focus our attention? How does it compare with other stories, metaphors and proverbs that were common in the time of Jesus? Does the parable evoke any themes from folklore or the Old Testament? What is the dynamics of the parable? The aesthetic approach suggests that we respond to a parable on many levels with our minds, with our feelings, and perhaps even with an unconscious resonance to its archetypal themes. Such levels of response are the ground of any conversion. They allow a new world of being in the presence of God to shape the lives of those who respond to them. An important element in the dynamics of many parables is their incompleteness. Jesus does not finish the story. The hearer must "fill in" what happens next. Often the way in which a person "fills in" the parable is a key to his or her presuppositions about God or humanity. We need to ask ourselves why we make one choice rather than another.

Since they have been handed down to us as part of the teaching of Jesus and of the early Church, the parables have been felt to have more than historical and literary interest. They claim to present a picture of human life that not only is true but is a key to the most important dimension of human life—its "being in the presence of" God as creator and redeemer. Since the parables focus on very ordinary human experience, they have a human significance. We need to ask what they show us about how humans live with each other. This dimension of the parables makes them applicable to "every person"—not just to first century Jewish farmers, merchants and the like. The human dimension is the foundation for the religious significance of the parables. Jesus has a vision of how people can live in the presence of God. The parables are part of his presentation of that vision and faith. They have a tragic undertone for the Christian reader who knows that that preaching would eventually lead to the fateful conflicts which precipitated Jesus' death. That conflict suggests that more is at stake than renewal of the ancient wisdom or prophecy of Israel. Jesus has challenged the world of meaning about humans and God that others thought firmly established [Meyer:162f]. The parables may also challenge some elements of "falsehood" in our own faith.

Why Speak in Parables? (Mk 4:10-12//Mt 13:10-17 (Lk 10:23f)//Lk 8:9f; Mk 4:21-25//Lk 8:16-18 (Mt 13:12); Mk 4:33f//Mt 13:34f)

We can see something of the various approaches in action by turning to the passages in the gospels which comment on the parable telling of Jesus. You will notice that the wording of the parallel passages is very close, much closer than one would expect for independent oral versions of the same material. Scholars usually proceed on the simplest assumption that Matthew and Luke had a version of Mark. We can compare each of them to Mark.

Look at Matthew's version. Verses 14–17 are typical of his composition. What Jesus has done is tied to a formal quotation from the prophets (vv. 14f). These verses clarify a prophetic allusion in the previous verse. Verses 16f add a beatitude which appears elsewhere in the tradition (Lk 10:23f). The beatitude sharpens the contrast between the disciples who accept the teaching of Jesus, the Messiah, and the others who do not. Verses 11 and 12 also show signs of reworking. Verse 12 relocates Mk 4:25 so that it becomes a comment on the knowledge that belongs to the disciples. The proverb in v. 11a is expanded so that it contrasts the disciples with others. Matthew's reworking of the passage heightens the judgmental aspect of the allusion to Is 6:9f in the Markan version. "Understanding/not understanding" the teaching of Jesus spells the difference between salvation and rejection. Matthew makes the theme of division and judgment the reason for parabolic speech. He will use this proverb again in a parable warning the Christian community that it too will be judged (25:29 = 13:12).

Luke's version is less elaborate. Some argue that he is deliberately softening a harsh Markan picture of the disciples. However, most of his revisions seem to be stylistic. He seeks to clarify the point of the section and has used the parable of the Sower independently of the longer collection in Mark/Matthew.

Analysis of Mark's version is more difficult, since we do not have sources that he may have used. Some interpreters begin by pointing to Mk 4:34 as evidence that mystery does not belong to the original purpose of the parable. Parables are intended to illuminate a point so that it becomes clear, not concealed. Mk 4:34f makes a distinction between Jesus' teaching of the crowds and of his own disciples. Disciples receive further instruction. They suggest that later Christians used that distinction to explain why Jesus was rejected. They embodied it in the picture of the parable as a deliberate attempt to conceal the message from outsiders that is found in Mk 4:10–12. Mark frequently points out the fear and misunderstanding of Jesus' own disciples. He wishes to point out that if they could overcome that weakness, then Christians of his day can also overcome their tribulations. Verse 13 and the warning in vv. 22–24 both imply that the disciples can understand the parable. Later in the gospel, they will be accused of the same hardness of heart mentioned in the prophecy (6:52; 8:21; 9:32).

While misunderstanding on the part of the disciples represents one of the themes of Mark's story, the saying in vv. 11f appears to be an independent, pre-Markan saying. The expression "mystery" was used in many Jewish writings to refer to knowledge of the plan by which God would bring this age to a close and inaugurate the new messianic age. Christians traditionally used the Isaiah passage to explain the rejection of Jesus by his people. Look at Rom 11:5-8. Paul uses that quote to explain the "mystery" (cf. v. 25) that the Jews and Gentiles seem to have switched places. People thought that the Jews would receive the Messiah, evil would be wiped out, and all the peoples of the earth would then come streaming to Jerusalem to worship God. Now it appears that the Gentiles have received the Messiah whom the Jews rejected. Paul hopes that the final result will be the streaming in of the Jews. Those who see Mk 4:11 as an early Jewish Christian explanation of Jesus' rejection point to the contrast between its exclusion of some people and Jesus' own attempts to include all. Mark's introduction deals with that difficulty. He contrasts those outside with those around Jesus. The latter group is different from the twelve. Thus, v. 10 suggests that the parable had divided the crowd. Some had left. Others had stayed with the group around Jesus. The further explanation is aimed at them.

Others argue that this view of parable telling may be ascribed to Jesus [Kermode:25-47]. The word "parable," *mashal,* means a riddle, an apocalyptic mystery as in v. 11, or a didactic story. Jesus may have been playing on the polarity riddle-didactic story. Later in the narrative Mark makes the disciples parallel to the outsiders so that both groups are involved in the effort to penetrate the enigma of Jesus' sayings. The passage in question embodies the correct perception that the parable both reveals and conceals at the same time. Enigma in Jesus' words need not be explained away as the result of the transmission of the tradition. They were not intended to be so clear that they would not require any effort of interpretation from the hearer. Thus, the possibility of fateful misunderstanding and rejection belongs to them from the beginning. Mark's narrative uses the parables as part of a greater enigma, that of Jesus' mission. Will he overcome the obstacles posed by the demons, the crowds, the misunderstanding of his own disciples, the hostility of Jewish authorities, to accomplish his mission as the suffering Son of Man? Will the parables be heard so that the one who has will receive more?

Mark has composed the passage so that it emphasizes the enigmatic:

Narrative Discourse:

> And when he was alone,
> they asked him—
> *those around him* with the twelve—
> about *the parables.*

Direct Discourse:

> And he said to them,
> To you the mystery has been given
> of the kingdom of God,
> but *to those outside,*
> in *parables* all things are
> lest . . . + OT allusion

The contrast "those around/those outside" frames the saying. The first group has the mystery of the kingdom; for the others all remains "in parables," that is, mysterious in a negative sense. These verses are not primarily concerned with the meaning of the parable of the Sower, which they follow. Instead, they force the reader to confront the larger question: What is the mystery

of the rule of God? The first answer to the question lies in the
allusion to Isaiah. Those outside lack perception. Those around
Jesus have "repented and he has healed them." The mystery,
then, is associated with the preaching of the kingdom and the
call for repentance (Mk 1:15). Mark's reader knows that the authority to forgive belongs to Jesus himself (2:1–12; 3:28f). He or
she can see that Jesus must be the source of forgiveness referred
to in Isaiah. Thus, the Markan scene associates parable telling,
the mystery of the kingdom, and the enigma of Jesus himself.
Only those around Jesus have caught on to what has been said
and have received the forgiveness that belongs to the coming of
the rule of God.

Mark then has to use v. 13 to move from this general scene
back to the interpretation of the Sower. Many scholars consider
it a veiled condemnation of the disciples, which is omitted by
Matthew/Luke. However, the rhetorical structure of the passage
suggests that the verse is not really addressed to "the twelve"
but to Mark's audience. He is concerned lest they put themselves
outside. You will notice that he follows the interpretation of the
Sower with a collection of Jesus' sayings which warn the Christian not to become slack in witnessing to what he or she knows
to be true about Jesus. This warning requires that one be careful
how one hears the message about Jesus. These warnings are introduced by v. 13. Matthew relocates the one saying that he uses
from that collection. Luke shortens the whole passage.

You will notice that Matthew has simplified the enigma of
the opening section. The disciples have been given *to know the
secrets;* the others have not. By using the plural "secrets" instead
of the singular, the enigma is no longer identified with Jesus
himself. Instead, "secrets" refers to the teaching of Jesus. Similarly, the connection between the prophecy and those who repent
is lost. Neither Matthew nor Luke contains the final phrase of
the Markan allusion. Matthew's formula quotation does include
the phrase about healing. He uses other quotations from Isaiah
to describe Jesus as the humble servant, come to heal God's people (12:16–21; 8:17). His readers would probably associate this
quotation with that picture of Jesus.

Luke also uses "mysteries" indicating a concern with the
teaching of Jesus. Some indication of the function of the scene in
Luke can be gleaned from his use of material in Mk 4:22–25.

Luke omits the concluding section in Mk 4:33f altogether, while Matthew has added a prophetic quote about the crowds to the first part and deferred the conclusion to 13:51 where it serves to check the disciples' understanding. By omitting this concluding section, Luke fits the interpretation of the Sower directly in with that on the true relatives of Jesus, those who "hear the word of God and do it." This description fits the elements of warning about how one hears the teaching of Jesus that Lk 8:16–18 retains from Mk 4:22–25. The section on true relatives of Jesus forms an inclusio with the motif introduced in 8:1–3, that of the women healed by Jesus, who were traveling with Jesus and providing financial support for the mission. The saying in v. 18b may have been used in the Lukan church to support the ethic of generous giving (cf. 6:38). Whatever a person gives will be amply rewarded as in the case of the Sower. Thus, the whole section sets up the behavior of the women as an example to the wealthy Christians in the congregation. The women are rewarded by being counted true relatives of Jesus.

Each evangelist has presented these sayings on speaking in parables to different issues in the audience. The parable as metaphorical speech demands a response to Jesus. The parable does not present factual information that a person can receive and remain neutral. The evangelists remind us that this engagement is intended to be an ongoing one. Becoming a Christian is not the end of the story. Christians must be reminded that they cannot become smug about their status as insiders who "know the secret." This secret is not knowledge to be remembered. It is a reality that is to reshape the whole life of the disciple. Those who "cannot hear" are not missing out on a piece of information. They are missing out on a whole way of life, which is salvation itself.

The discussion of parabolic speech in this passage does not mean to encourage Christians to fatalistic passivity—those who do not believe are fated to do so. The sayings about the necessity of Christian witness in 4:22–25 guard against that view. But this section does point to a motif which runs throughout the Bible. God offers salvation in such a way that people must turn to him in order to receive it. He never forces salvation on his people. As a result, salvation is decided in certain fate-full moments of hearing the word of God. Concealment is not some malicious ambiguity on God's part. Rather, it protects this necessary dynamics of biblical faith: people must turn to God for healing.

Classifying Parables

This excursion into the richness of parabolic language makes it obvious that any attempt to classify the parables will have its problems. Any number of literary, thematic and theological schemes have been proposed. Some parables are simple proverbs or analogies which compare one thing with another. Others involve short narratives of some typical but slightly unusual situation. Unlike the analogies, the comparison is not simply between the rule of God and something else. It is between the topic about which Jesus speaks and "what happens," the whole action of the story. Still other stories may have been crafted as examples of some point of the teaching of Jesus so that the hearer can "get a feel for" what acting according to that teaching would involve. We will suggest a threefold grouping of the parables. This grouping does not exhaust all the possibilities for classifying the parables. It is simply a suggestion to provide a map of the terrain before we plunge into it.

Our first group comprises parables that either are proverbial sayings or seem to have been expanded from proverbs. Some of the action-response parables in the next section are also related to proverbs, but they have been turned in the direction of narrative dynamics rather than proverbial observation.

Fig. 1: PARABLES DERIVED FROM PROVERBS

PROVERBIAL SAYINGS:	PROVERBS EXPANDED IN THE DIRECTION OF NARRATIVE:	
	common experience	*as warning/judgment*
patched garment/wine skins (Mk 2:21f par)	two debtors (Lk 7:41ff)	children in the market (Mt 11:16–19//Lk 7:31–35)
lamp (Mk 4:21 par)	closed door (Lk 13:25)	seine net (Mt 13:47f)
salt (Mk 9:50 par)	servant's life (Lk 17:7–10)	unclean spirit (Mt 12:43–45//Lk 11:24–26)
strong man (Mk 3:27 par)	way to judgment (Lk 12:58//Mt 5:25f)	man with two sons (Mt 21:28–32)

Fig. 2: PARABLES OF DISCOVERY AND RESPONSE

ADVENT:

(These parables emphasize the rule of God as recasting the future.)

hiddenness/mystery	*gift/surprise*	*discovery/joy*
fig tree (Mk 13:28 par)	sower (Mk 4:3–8 par)	lost sheep (Mt 18:12f//Lk 15:3–7)
leaven (Mk 13:33 par)	mustard seed (Mk 4:30–32 par)	lost coin (Lk 15:8f)
seed growing secretly (Mk 4:24–26)	treasure (Mt 13:44)	
wheat and tares (Mt 13:24–30)	pearl (Mt 13:45f)	

ACTION

(These parables focus on action in crucial situations.)

adequate	*failed*
friend at midnight (Lk 11:5–8)	rich fool (Lk 12:16–20)
unjust judge (Lk 18:2–5)	wedding garment (Mt 22:11–14)

While the proverbial type depends upon astute observation of common situations for its effectiveness, other parables present action in situations that are unique or unexpected. The hearer may never find him or herself in such a situation but can learn from the action presented. The unusual features of these stories capture our attention.

The plot of the parables in this group remains relatively simple. A single figure either takes effective action in the situation or fails to do so. The Advent type also includes some analogies from natural processes, which might be related to the proverbial type. However, these parables do not represent conventional wisdom. They turn on a surprising abundance or growth which is out of proportion with the effort expended by humans.

The final group represents more extended narrative. Most involve the fate of more than one character. Their responses highlight the fatefulness of one's encounter with the word of God. Some of the shorter parables in each category might be de-

Fig. 3:   NARRATIVE PARABLES

REVERSAL OF STATUS:
(These parables reverse common positions on status. Most serve as ethical examples in Luke.)

guests (Lk 14:7–14)   first seats/last seats
Pharisee/publican (Lk 18:10–14)   pious/sinner
good Samaritan (Lk 10:30–37)   priest, Levite (religious Jew)/non-
                                                          Jew (irreligious enemy)
great supper (Lk 14:16–24//Mt
22:1–10)   invited/uninvited—able
rich man/Lazarus (Lk 16:19–31)   rich/poor
prodigal son (Lk 15:11–32)   dutiful/prodigal

SERVANT PARABLES:
(This group represents masters and servants in crisis situations.)

Type I: Command—Departure—Action—Return—Reward/Punishment,
as expected
doorkeeper (Mt 13:33–37 par)
good steward (Mt 24:45–51//Lk 12:42–46)
throne claimant (Lk 19:12b, 14–15a, 27)
talents (Mt 25:14–30//Lk 19:12–26)
wise/foolish virgins (Mt 25:1–13)

Type II: Reward/Punishment contain unexpected elements
(This group may be said to explore the limits of the first type.)
unmerciful servant (Mt 18:23–28)
vineyard workers (Mt 20:1–13)
wicked tenants (Mk 12:1–9 par)
unjust steward (Lk 16:1–8)

---

rived from one of the earlier types. We include them here because they seem designed to set up some of the categories that are behind the longer stories [also see Crossan, 1973:75–77].

These three charts will give you some idea of the range of Jesus' parables. "Par" indicates those which appear in all three synoptic gospels. Others appear in Matthew/Luke and may have been part of a collection of teachings of Jesus that these evangelists shared, which scholars call "Q." Still others appear in only one gospel. Interpretation of the individual parables will enable us to see the complexity of the stories, which cannot be grasped in this simple scheme. You can also see that the parables address varied dimensions of discipleship. A certain "conversion" to Jesus' point of view might even be said to be required by some of them, though their roots in common experience and use of everyday language make them potentially accessible to all. One does not need to master an esoteric or technical religious vocabulary in order to appreciate the parables. In that respect, parables are like Jesus himself, available to all men, women, children, sinners, Gentiles. But accessibility does not mean that a parable is like a TV ad, designed to force its message on you even when you are trying not to listen. The parable demands that we become involved in the process in order to understand. The hearer has to make some fundamental decisions about the meaning of the parable.

Summary

The dynamics of parable telling and hearing would seem to make writing a book such as this something of a contradiction. The book cannot stand between the reader and the parable without undermining the very speech that it seeks to clarify and make accessible. Students are sometimes offended by the various dimensions of the parable. They would prefer simple meanings that could be learned. Or, they would like to confine their study to the historical and religious background from the time of Jesus. They find the aesthetic appreciation of the parables more difficult. Such demands are typical of a fact-oriented culture. Certainly, we need some information in order to appreciate the situations represented in the parables. But we cannot enter into the dynamics of the parable if we simply ask informational questions. We need to appreciate the special vision and creativity in the parables of Jesus. We need to explore the wide range of human experiences presented in the parables. Perhaps we need to look at our own experience to see how the experiences in the parables address us. These dimensions of the parable draw upon our resources of imagination and sensitivity. Many of the parables even challenge us to create our own conclusions about the story which is half finished. This demand means that we have to appreciate both what leads us to complete the story in one way and what leads another person to a different conclusion. In short, we have to participate in the process of parable telling. Christians will ask what the challenge of Jesus' faith as presented through the parables has to say to their situation today. But even those who do not feel a strong identification with any religious group, or the increasing group of those who are wondering if in throwing out religion they have missed something, may begin asking about the picture of human life presented in the parables. The parables engage us in religious questions in a fashion that is still open to our humanity; they do not demand complete conversion first. After all, we can always remember that first audience of Jesus—interested, skeptical, hostile. The outsiders also listened and the parables sought to address them (Mk 4:33).

STUDY QUESTIONS

1. How is Jesus' experience of faith represented in parables?

2. How were the parables handed down to us? What is the difference between the original audience of the parables and the readers envisaged by the gospels?

3. Describe the four approaches to interpreting a parable.

4. What lesson did Matthew draw from his study of Mk 4:10–12 for Christians? What lesson did Luke draw from the passage?

5. What does the word *mashal* (parable) mean?

6. How does Mark relate the "mystery of the kingdom of God" to Jesus himself?

7. Why is it difficult to classify parables?

8. What does the parable demand of the person who hears it?

Chapter One

WHAT'S IN A PARABLE?

Parables and the Modern Imagination

A collection of modern parables is entitled "Imperial Messages" [Schwartz:1976]. The contents show that many of our most distinguished writers have been exploring the parable genre. The title is taken from a parable by Franz Kafka. A dying emperor, surrounded by throngs, sends "you" a message. But the emperor is in a vast palace so packed with people that even with the imperial seal on his chest the messenger could hardly reach the gate. And, if he were to get that far,

> the imperial capital would lie before him, the center of the world, crammed to bursting with its own sediment. Nobody would fight his way through here even with a message from a dead man. But you sit at your window when evening falls and dream it to yourself.
>
> (Schwartz:2)

The twentieth century heritage of this parable is obvious. People no longer live in an age that receives messages from distant powers. Too much sediment lies between us and any transcendent

15

sources of order. The best we can hope for is a daydream at dusk. The story also makes the power of the parable genre clear. In a short space, it evokes the whole mood of a world. No one can miss the overtones of wistful sadness. Yet the finality and closure of its vision is equally clear. No miracle will change the situation. The emperor is dead.

Others have compared Jesus' parables to Zen koans, those enigmatic words and actions by which Zen masters seek to awaken their students to an experience of self/reality beyond all the imprisoning bonds of life and ego structure. Here is a koan that focuses on a traditional poem about nature:

> A monk once asked Master Fuketsu, "Both speaking and silence are concerned with ri-bi relativity. How can we be free and non-transgressing?" Fuketsu said:
> How fondly I remember Konan in March!
> The partridges are calling, and the flowers are fragrant.
>
> (Shibayama:175)

Even the reader who is not a Zen student can sense the authentic vision and power of the master's response. Note the typical Zen appeal to the concrete, what's under your nose: Look! See!

You can see from our survey in the Introduction that both kings/masters and nature analogies are frequent subjects of Jesus' parables. He directs our attention to the every day. The parables imply that our destiny is at stake in ordinary domestic, economic and social existence [see Wilder, 1971:74]. Like the Zen example, Jesus' parables are short and sharply focused. By contrast, modern authors usually run a page or more and use symbolism. Many have dimensions of the "unreal," the fable, the legend, the fairy tale—all lost worlds. Jesus on the other hand often points our attention with expressions like "now" and "which of you?" He has no nostalgia for a world that he cannot recover but points us to the world at hand.

Wilder warns against letting the modern imagination dictate our reading of the Bible. Private experience or individual enlightenment does not capture the reality of biblical salvation. Salvation must be won in the social and public realm. Jesus was struggling for the social imagination of his audience. He sought to change some of the loyalties, common assumptions and barriers that kept people from recognizing the presence and action of God. Then they could see themselves as having a share in the final purification of the people and the blessing that God's presence would bring to all creation. Jesus was not engaged in the modern preoccupation with overthrowing traditions and authorities. He was not preaching individual transcendence or imagining a nostalgic return to some less complicated past [Wilder, 1976:11–40].

The Challenge of the Rule of God

The expression "rule of God" can symbolize some fundamental concepts of biblical religion. There humans live in a world which is not at their own disposal, since it is not the product of impersonal forces. They live in the world at the pleasure of its creator. The legal and ethical traditions of Israel embody that relationship. God is their king and savior. They must acknowledge his sovereignty to the exclusion of all other gods and kings. They must actualize his justice in special concern for all members of the society. Every Jew knew that the story of Israel had been one of repeated summons back to the Lord from false gods, from social evils, and even from false confidence in the protection of God. God is not just a supreme king and creator who punishes his disobedient people. He is like a father (sometimes mother) with his children, a shepherd with sheep, a husband with an unfaithful wife—always coaxing, pleading, seeking to awaken in the people the love he feels for them.

Some of Jesus' contemporaries felt that the record of disobedience was so bad that they withdrew into sects which tried to obey God's Law with special intensity. The Essenes, for example, had an initiation ceremony in which a person first confessed the sinfulness of Israel and then promised obedience, thanking God for the holiness of the sect:

> All who join the Covenant shall make their confession after them (=the priests), saying: "We have sinned; we have rebelled. We have sinned; we have done evil, we and our fathers before us, by transgressing the true precepts. God is just, who has fulfilled his judgment against

us and our fathers. But he extends his mercy toward us
forever and ever." And the priests shall bless all the
men of the lot of God (= Essenes), who walk perfectly
in all his ways.

(Community Rule I, 24—II, 2)

Others may not have joined such sects, but they felt the general pessimism about human nature that we find reflected in the wisdom literature. Ecclesiastes is a well-known example. Consider this parable:

I have also seen this example of wisdom under the sun,
and it seemed great to me. There was a little city with
few men in it; and a great king came against it and be-
sieged it, building great siegeworks against it. But there
was found in it a poor, wise man, and he by his wisdom
delivered the city. Yet no one remembered the poor
man. But I say that wisdom is better than might, though
the poor man's wisdom is despised, and his words are
not heeded.

(9:13-16)

The wise person may be able to avoid the vanity that drives the rest of the world. Here, Ben Sirach describes the lot of the poor:

When a rich man totters, he is steadied by friends,
    but when a humble man falls, he is even pushed away
        by friends.
If a rich man slips, his helpers are many;
    he speaks unseemly words, and they justify him.
If a humble man slips, they even reproach him;
    he speaks sensibly and receives no attention.
When the rich man speaks all are silent,
    and they extol to the clouds what he has to say.
When the poor man speaks they say, "Who is this fel-
    low?"
    And should he stumble, they even push him down.

(13:21-23)

The same author recognizes that God the creator acts out of compassion for his weak, sinful and short-lived creature:

> He who lives forever created the whole universe;
>   the Lord alone will be declared righteous.
> To none has he given power to proclaim his works;
>   and who can search out his mighty deeds?
> Who can measure his majestic power?
>   And who can fully recount his mercies?
> It is not possible to diminish or increase them,
>   nor is it possible to trace the wonders of the Lord.
> When a man has finished, he is just beginning,
>   and when he stops, he will be at a loss.
> What is man, and of what use is he?
>   What is his good, and what is his evil?
> The number of a man's days is great
>   if he reaches a hundred years.
> Like a drop of water in the sea, and a grain of sand,
>   so are a few years in the day of eternity.
> Therefore the Lord is patient with them,
>   and pours out his mercy upon them.
> He sees and recognizes that their end will be evil;
>   therefore he grants them forgiveness in abundance.
> The compassion of man is for his neighbor,
>   but the compassion of the Lord is for all living things.
> He rebukes and trains and teaches them,
>   and turns them back as a shepherd his flock.
> He has compassion on those who accept his discipline
>   and who are eager for his judgments.
>
> (18:1-14)

The wisdom tradition seeks to encourage love of the Law, humility, compassion for the poor and justice in the face of a realistic and rather negative picture of "the way the world is." The striking contrast between the frailty and mortality of humans and the greatness of God the creator should inspire gratitude for his mercy.

Jewish apocalyptic writings, which claimed to be ancient prophecies of the history and end of the world, portrayed their time as one of great evil. It would soon be brought to an end by God's cosmic intervention and his judgment against sinful humanity. IV Ezra, an apocalypse from the first century A.D., laments the wickedness of humanity while the revealing angel points to the few who will be saved. Here is an exchange which includes a parable of a sower:

"For in this, Lord, your righteousness and goodness will be declared, if you will be compassionate toward those who have no wealth of good works." He (= the angel) answered, "Some of what you have said is right and will happen. Indeed, I will not be concerned about the creation of those who have sinned, or about their death, judgment or damnation. Rather, I will rejoice over the creation of the righteous, over their pilgrimage, their salvation and their reward. It will be as you have said. For, just as the farmer sows much seed on the ground and plants many plants, and yet not all that were sown will be saved at the harvest, nor will all that is planted take root; so also those sown in the world will not all be saved." I replied, "If I have found favor with you, let me speak. If the farmer's seed does not come up—because it has not received your rain at the right time—or, if it is ruined by too much rain, it dies; but humans who are made by your own hands and in your own image, for whom you made all things, are you comparing them to a farmer's seed? No, Lord God! Spare your people, and have compassion on your inheritance, for you are compassionate toward all your creation."
He answered, "Compare present with present and future with future. You are far from loving my creation more than I! Many times have you interceded for the wicked, 'This must not be!' But even for that you will be honored before God because you humbled yourself and did not assign yourself a place among the righteous, and so you will receive the greater glory, unlike those who live in the world in the last days, because they walked in pride. But consider your own case and those who are like you; search out their glory. For you Paradise is open; the tree of life, planted; the future age made

ready, and bounty prepared. . . . Therefore, stop asking
about the multitude of people who perish, for, having
been given freedom, they despised the Law of the Most
High, forsook his ways, trampled his saints under foot,
and have said in their heart, 'There is no God'—even
though they knew they would have to die . . . so thirst
and anguish await them. For the Most High did not will
humans to be destroyed; but they—his creatures—have
themselves defiled the name of the One who made them,
and shown themselves ungrateful to the One who prepared life for them. Therefore, my judgment is now at
hand; and I have not made this known to all people, but
only to you and to a few like you."

(8:36–62)

The only consolation given the seer is confidence in the reward
that does await the few who are righteous and assurance that
God's judgment is finally at hand. The next quotation comes
from a first century B.C. writing. It describes the final judgment
as his kingdom. Salvation exalts Israel over her enemies:

Then his kingdom will appear in all his creation. Then
Satan will be no more, and sorrow will depart with him.
Then the hands of the archangel will be filled, and he
will immediately avenge them against their enemies.
For the Heavenly One will arise from his royal throne,
and he will go forth from his holy habitation with indig-
nation and wrath on account of his sons. The earth will
tremble, be shaken to its depths. The high mountains
will be made low, and the hills shaken and fall. The
horns of the sun will be broken and it will be turned into
darkness. The moon will not give light, and will be
turned to blood. The circle of the stars will be disturbed,
the sea retire into the abyss, the fountains of water fail,
and the rivers dry up. For the Most High will arise, the
Eternal God alone. He will appear to punish the Gentiles, and he will destroy all their idols. And you, O Israel, will be happy. You will mount on the neck and
wings of the eagle. They will be abolished, and God will
exalt you. He will bring you up to the starry heaven.

> You will look from on high and see your enemies in Ge-
> henna. You will recognize them and rejoice. You will
> give thanks and bless your creator.
> (Assumption of Moses 10:1–10)

Here, God's rule appears in a cosmic judgment that shows the creator to be protecting his people. The Gentiles who have held them in subjection will be punished.

A whole complex of religious issues were focused around the question of God's rule and judgment. Perhaps, some who heard that Jesus spoke of the kingdom of God thought of the military images of national exaltation. Others might have looked for something more along the lines of IV Ezra, a special revelation to assure the righteous that God would indeed save them. Jesus does not respond to the religious dilemmas expressed in these writings in the same vein. Rather, he seeks to give his people a different vision of God, his justice, his presence and his relationship to creation. This vision is to dissolve such dilemmas.

The Scale of the Kingdom

One key to this reorientation lies in a change of scale. Both wisdom and apocalyptic operate on a "cosmic" scale when speaking about the power of God. Not so Jesus. One scholar compares the parables to "home movies" made around some of the grand themes celebrated in this literature [Breech:17–24, 35]. The solution that the wise men and seers thought required a cosmic scale could be found right under our noses. The parables often take Old Testament symbols and reduce them to an individual level— not God and the nation, just a single shepherd and a flock. This reduction even leads some to claim that Jesus is not alluding to the Old Testament images at all.

Another facet of the reduction in scale is focus on the individual and on particular situations. The wisdom statements about rich and poor could apply to any persons, anywhere. The parables, on the other hand, present individuals in rather unique situations. When early Christian preachers wanted to apply Jesus' parables to more general teaching, they frequently added sayings onto the end of the story. These sayings provide the parable with a more universal point or application.

Some of the rabbinic parables are also on the individual

scale of Jesus' stories, but they are firmly anchored to teaching about observance of the Law. The moral lesson is never far from the story as in the following parable, which was told to illustrate the relations between the Israelites and the Egyptians in Exodus 14:5:

> Rabbi Şimon says in a parable: To what can this be compared? To a man who had inherited property in a distant country, which he sold for very little. But, the buyer went and discovered in the house treasures, stores of silver, gold, precious stones and pearls. When the seller saw this, he began to choke with grief; so also did the Egyptians . . . + OT quote
>
> (Mekilta Exodus 14:5)

Another version attributed to the same rabbi compares the Egyptians to a man who had inherited a dung heap. Since he was lazy he sold it, but the industrious purchaser dug in it and found a treasure. He was able to go around like a rich person. Then the seller began to choke and lament what he had thrown away [Jeremias:32]. This version has an additional moral lesson: laziness does the original owner out of the treasure.

Jesus' stories are usually not as simple. Exaggerations and ambiguities make it difficult to nail the point of the story down. Jesus' treasure story (Mt 13:44) has the man find the treasure in someone else's field, rebury it, and buy the field. Jewish law would have required that he divide the treasure with the original owner under such circumstances [Crossan, 1979:67–71]. Jesus' story does not provide any reason for the original owner to have lost out on his treasure. The legal traditions even suggest that the truly pious person will not wait for the owner to initiate a suit to gain his share of the treasure but will voluntarily divide it with him. (The cases all assume that the buyer did not know the field contained treasure.) Jesus' story may be closer to what we would expect a person to do in such a situation, but it leaves us with several questions.

The rabbinic examples suggest that there may have been a common tale about such treasure in circulation. Folktales from many parts of the world concern buried treasures [Crossan, 1979]. Not surprisingly, the Jewish tales reflect ethical and religious values: the poor, pious and industrious deserve the treasure as reward. Other cultures structure such tales around their own values. The heroes usually are disadvantaged members of society, the youngest son, the widow or orphan, the poor man with a large family, the ugly stepdaughter, or the fool. Such people are felt to deserve the treasure. Sometimes the finder's inability to obtain or use the treasure wisely serves as a warning against greed or other vices. Jesus' story is not quite like such a folktale. It does not represent common social values. It is also much shorter. Folktales were told to entertain. Descriptions, thwarted plans and other subplots provide the enjoyment of a "good story." In addition, many contain elements of the "unreal," the world of magical aid. The lessons and values they imprint on the imagination of the audience do not come through characters one might expect to encounter in everyday life.

By comparison, the realism of Jesus' stories also appears to reduce their scale. Some commentators are led by it into supposing that Jesus is commenting on local events. Such views usually run up against the incongruous elements in the stories which make it impossible to find a direct social or legal parallel. The magical atmosphere of the folktale makes it clear that one is not to make such a mistake. Jesus' parables, on the other hand, invite us to do so. The brevity and economy of speech in Jesus' stories contributes to this impression. Sometimes one has the feeling that one is reading only the synopsis of a story such as one finds in early collections of folklore that compressed longer stories into summaries. This brevity often contributes to the ambiguity of the story. The details we supply as readers may be related to the stories we have heard as children. This brevity reminds us that Jesus' parables are part of a larger context of speech like the rabbinic example. Jesus does not come as a singer of tales for the sake of the tale. Rather, the parable is subordinate to other forms of speech in which he presents his message about the rule of God.

The Parables in the Gospels

The parables are part of a different context in the synoptic gospels. There they are handed on within the context of early Christian preaching. Rules of conduct are derived from them. The parables are interpreted within the context of Jesus' own

Fig. 4:   CHARACTERISTICS OF THE SYNOPTIC PARABLES

	MATTHEW	MARK	LUKE
WORLD	men and their activities	nature	ordinary men and women of means
SCALE	grand, ostentatious	village	town, local notables
CONTRASTS	black and white, stock characters	no clear use of it	not in principle; can use uncontrasted figures
ALLEGORY	frequent in long parables	occasional details	in material shared with Mt/Mk, Luke's special material is not allegorical
RESPONSE	Mt/Mk: God is presenting the final challenge; be prepared Matthew occasionally adds exhortation to specify the response.		ethical conclusions aimed at Christian teaching
COMPARISON	Mt/Mk: Compare things that are alike in some way; "if 'x', then how much the more 'y'."		frequently will compare like with unlike, i.e. God: suppliant = unjust judge:widow
APPEAL	Mt/Mk: Use indirect opening; may conclude with direct command of the Lord		Likes direct opening, "which of you?" and direct discourse within the story.

fate. Or they are employed as warnings about the conduct required for those who would be saved in the impending judgment. Sometimes specific characters are identified with Jesus, God, and the Jews, and so the parable is turned into an allegory. Early Christian preachers may have collected parables according to theme such as the collection of seed parables in Mark 4. Parables are often given generalizing conclusions which refer to judgment [Jeremias:110–112]. Such conclusions might be said to be the final call to remind the audience to apply the teaching of the parable. The form of the parable itself invites such application, since it calls upon the audience to decide what the story means. In so doing, one may pronounce judgment on oneself.

Others have tried to sketch the differences in the parables told by each gospel writer [Gouldner, 1968]. Figure 4 will give you a general picture of their results.

Some of the differences derive from the traditions used by the different authors. Each evangelist emphasizes what is suited to the situation of his community. Luke might even be said to contribute to the dramatic power of some stories by his use of direct discourse rather than the indirect third person of the variant. He seems to recognize that the judgment of the world is not around the corner and so turns to parables whose ethical application can serve to instruct the well-off, educated Christians of his community.

Similes for the Rule of God

Our first group of parables contains short similes for the rule of God. The only synoptic versions are in Mt 13:44–48. GTh provides second century versions. There, the stories are not connected, so we may assume that they circulated independently of one another. Matthew may have grouped them and added verses 49f to the Net as a conclusion for the whole group. All three raise questions about the focus of the comparison. Is it the object found (value), the action taken by the finder to obtain the object, or the response to the discovery (joy)?

The Treasure (Mt 13:44//GTh 109)

We have seen that some other versions of the treasure story suggest conclusions which an audience might supply. Perhaps the finder will show off his wealth. Perhaps the original owner will file suit to obtain the share of the treasure due him. One Jewish story resolves the problem by having the finder's son marry the owner's daughter [Jeremias:200]. The Jewish philosopher Philo compares the householder who suddenly finds a treasure in his field to a person who discovers wisdom [Crossan, 1979:64ff]. Perhaps the audience would expect a religious allegory. Jesus' parable does not provide us with answers to these possibilities. GTh 109, on the other hand, has a variant of the Jewish folk tradition:

> The kingdom is like a man who had a treasure hidden in his field without knowing it. He died and left it to his son, who took the field and sold it. The buyer came and found the treasure while ploughing. He began to lend money at interest to anyone he wished.

True to the folklore pattern, the finder demonstrates his new wealth.

Since Jesus' story stops with the finder buying the field, we may assume that the action is the focus of the story. Joy functions as a motivation for the action. It removes the story from the realm of legal niceties about ownership. Jesus does not suggest a form of behavior which transcends the Law; he wants us to concentrate on something different from the other versions of the story. Since the man did not own the field, we might assume that he is a laborer, who was too poor to own land of his own—or at least not enough of it to provide for his family. Such a person would literally have to sell everything in order to buy the field. Sometimes today an Egyptian village boy will decide to sell his ancestral plot to buy a taxi. He hopes to get rich taking tourists around to see the ancient monuments. Such decisions cause an uproar in the village, where land is still the most important thing a peasant can have. The common view is that any parting with one's land is courting disaster. Imagine Jesus' story on the scale of the village—where no behavior goes unnoticed or uncommented upon. The man's action is not trivial even though he does have the motive of the buried treasure. To gain the field, he has had to part with the very substance and security of his life. In addition, the audience knows that the original owner may well sue for part of the treasure. Since the man has sold everything, he will not be able to hide his sudden wealth. What will he do? What do you think happened?

Jesus' story is not as simple as it seems. A cautious person might well not act as this man has done. What little he has would be more security than the treasure. Or would it? What things do we hold onto with such peasant-like tenacity? What would get us to loosen our hold? The story is not a direct command to sell everything. It presents a striking image of a case in which a person is willing to really change everything about his life. Thus, it can be seen as a positive affirmation of the power of the presence of God to transform our lives. The man does not act out of the kind of calculation, or miscalculation, that the village boy does. He responds to an unexpected discovery. That discovery made it possible for him to launch out beyond the socially ingrained securities of his life. The rule of God is presented as the kind of thing that can provoke such action from those who discover it.

The Pearl (Mt 13:45f//GTh 76)

The structure of this parable is almost identical with the previous one. However, a merchant does not require motivation to act as he does. Pearls were traded for very large sums. Such extreme risks were part of the business. The stakes were as high in antiquity as they are in "high finance" today, and considerably more risk was involved, since the various forms of regulation and insurance that we have to guard against colossal disasters did not exist. Huge fortunes could be at stake in a single venture. Most of us could not even imagine taking such risks. Yet this story seems to intensify the risk-taking attitude of the previous one. The rule of God does not permit one to "play it safe."

GTh 76 changes the point. The merchant suddenly becomes a prudent business person:

> The kingdom of the Father is like a merchant who had goods and found a pearl. The merchant was prudent so he sold the goods and bought the pearl for himself. You too must seek for treasure which does not perish, which is where no moth comes to eat, and no worm destroys.

You can also see that the Christian preacher has been at work. A saying (Lk 12:33f par) has been added to present the point of the parable. Luke introduces the same saying with the injunction to "sell all." He sought to encourage wealthy Christians to help the poor. GTh comes from an area in which people often sought to imitate Jesus by a life of wandering asceticism. This parable and its interpretation are a call for that life: sell all to obtain salvation.

The Net (Mt 13:47f//GTh 8)

This parable is somewhat different, since the focus of comparison is the contents rather than the action. GTh 8 contains a fish story, which is more closely modeled on the Treasure and the Pearl:

> Man is like a wise fisherman casting his net into the sea. He drew it out full of little fish. Among them the wise fisherman found a large, good fish. The wise fisherman cast the little fish back into the sea and chose the large fish without difficulty.

Use what you have learned about GTh to interpret this version.

Jesus' description of the fish in the net responds to a different question. Remember IV Ezra? The number of evil people in the world had led him to question God's compassion. He thought that God should defend his own honor by rectifying the situation. How would Jesus' parable answer IV Ezra?

Matthew attaches a warning about judgment to the Net to serve as a conclusion for the group. Such warnings are typical of him. Each of the five discourses in the gospel concludes with words of warning (7:24–27; 10:40–42, a promise of reward; this section concludes the parables discourse of chapter 13; 18:34; 25:31–46). The delay in the judgment seems to have led some Christians in Matthew's church to become lax. He is constantly warning them to be ready for the judgment whenever it comes.

Lost Sheep (Mt 18:12–14//Lk 15:4–7//GTh 107)

GTh 107 provides another version of a parable which Matthew/Luke seem to have derived from Q. Compare the three versions given in Figure 5.

Fig. 5:   PARALLEL VERSIONS OF THE LOST SHEEP

MATTHEW	LUKE	GTH
See that you do not despise one of these little ones; for I tell you that in heaven their angels always behold the face of my Father in heaven.		
What do you think? If a man has a hundred sheep, and one of them has gone astray,	So he told them this parable, What man of you, having a hundred sheep, if he has lost one of them,	Jesus said, The kingdom is like a shepherd who had a hundred sheep. One of them went astray; it was the largest.
does he not leave the ninety-nine on the hills,	does not leave the ninety-nine in the wilderness,	He left the ninety-nine
and go in search of the one that went astray?	and go after the one which is lost,	and sought for the one
And if he finds it,	until he finds it?	until he found it.
truly I say to you, he rejoices over it more than over the ninety-nine that never went astray.	And when he has found it, he lays it on his shoulders, rejoicing.	
	And when he comes home, he calls together his friends and neighbors, saying to them, "Rejoice with me, for I have found my sheep, which was lost."	After he had exerted himself, he said to the sheep, "I love you more than the ninety-nine."
So it is not the will of my Father in heaven that one of these little ones should perish.	Just so I tell you, there will be more joy in heaven over one sinner who repents than over ninety-nine righteous persons who have no need of repentance.	

You can see that GTh has omitted some of the details of the story common to Matthew/Luke. It has also provided a reason for the shepherd's unusual action.

The shepherd leaves ninety-nine sheep alone while looking for the lost one. The introduction to the parable is formulated in such a way as to imply a negative answer: no one in the audience would do what this shepherd does. Some interpreters supply explanations to "fix up" that peculiarity—for example, he did not discover the loss until putting the sheep in the fold for the night. GTh has solved the problem by saying that the missing sheep was the largest and most beloved. We have already seen from the similes that prudent action is hardly a feature of the parables. Yet the emotion of the discovery might lead a person to act as this shepherd does. One might be so lucky as to find the others still there on one's return. Notice that Matthew even leaves the actual finding of such a lost sheep an open question.

Each evangelist uses the parable to teach a different lesson. Matthew uses it to warn Christian leaders that they must extend their concern to every member of the community. The sayings which frame the parable show that God's concern and care extend to every individual. Luke, on the other hand, stresses the motif of repentance and forgiveness. Both applications have some relation to the probable context for such a parable in the ministry of Jesus: his own concern for sinners and outcasts. Remember that "sinners" in the biblical context does not refer to good people who slip up once in a while. Rituals of atonement could restore them to God's favor. Sinners are those who deliberately choose to ignore the Law of God either through passive neglect, outright scorn, or even persecution of those who are trying to follow it. Perhaps you can see why Jesus' concern for such people was a matter of comment. Both the Essenes and IV Ezra console the righteous by reminding them that the sinners who think that they are "getting away with it" will soon hear from God in the judgment. Jesus' attitude seems quite different. The saying in Lk 15:7 and Mt 18:14 may also have expressed Jesus' answer to someone like IV Ezra who thought that the number of sinners was somehow an affront to God. Jesus insists that God does not will anyone to perish. His concern and compassion is not lacking—as IV Ezra had hinted. If anything, it is extravagant.

The Old Testament pictures God as a shepherd. He will seek the person who has strayed but who remembers his commandments the way a shepherd remembers a lost sheep (Ps 119:176). Sir 18:13 pictured God as the compassionate shepherd who turns the flock to the right path. The prophets use the image against the leaders of the people as bad shepherds. God will send new ones (Jer 23:1–4). Ez 34 has the sheep pray to God that God will relieve them of bad shepherds who have not searched for the lost. God promises that he himself will shepherd Israel and will set up the true Davidic king. Then there will be a time of messianic peace when all will know the presence of God: "I am with them." Jesus' parable fits into this tradition, but it has a slight twist. It does not require a change in the circumstances of the nation as a whole. Instead, it suggests that that hope might be recognized in the lives of individuals touched by the healing ministry of Jesus. Such a suggestion explodes a rigid application of the God as shepherd equation, which could only see God's shepherding presence in the large-scale destruction of sinners and bad human shepherds. Instead, God is the most imprudent of shepherds. The righteous can do quite well on their own. (Remember that this story does not condemn those good people who do not need to repent any more than it condemns the sheep who did not get lost.) God may even seem to leave the righteous to seek out the lost. Divine compassion is not a matter of prudent statistics. Better to take the loss of one sheep than risk losing the others. Still less will it accept an accommodation like that suggested in IV Ezra: loss of the majority is more than made up for by the sterling quality of the righteous who are saved.

Lost Coin (Lk 15:8-10)

Luke has an additional parable paired with the Lost Sheep. Like the Treasure/Pearl pair in Matthew, it explores the attitude of the actor and is less complex than the first parable. The woman is not risking losing another coin in her search, and she might well be expected to succeed. What seems to be important is the complete dedication to finding the coin; it drives out all other concerns. All her neighbors in the village hear her shout for joy. Some commentators try to explain her concern by saying that she had lost one of the coins from her dowry. Such an addition is not necessary in the context of a peasant village where any coins are the exception rather than the rule. Nor are we immune to such tailspins. A woman ahead of me in a supermarket checkout line found she was missing ten dollars she thought she had when she went to pay for her groceries. Though she did not need the money to pay, she kept all of us in line waiting while she went throught the entire contents of a large purse and located the missing bill. She then had to put it all back, of course, costing the rest of us twenty-five minutes on a busy Saturday morning. We were not exactly in the mood to rejoice when she found it either! And such a woman is what God/Jesus/the disciple is like when seeking out the lost!

Summary

A parable does not have to be very long to present a striking image of humans and their relationship with God. Though many are unusual events, all could well occur in everyday life. There could be such a laborer or shepherd; certainly there are such merchants, fishermen and housewives. We must not let our distance from village life in the first century turn the parables into romantic stories. They are not. Perhaps Jesus' audience knew someone in their village "just like" one of these characters and smiled with the same amusement I get from an audience when I tell the supermarket story.

The parable is not just an amusing incident—even when it served as an explanation to my husband for a delayed breakfast. Jesus is explaining what the rule and presence of God are like. He is taking sides on sensitive religious issues in a language that is for everyone—not just the few righteous as in the revelation in IV Ezra. Jesus points to the experiences of every villager. Learn from that, he suggests. But is it all so simple? Do we want to adopt the kind of behavior imaged in these stories? Do we want other people to do so? Do we want God to? Or do we really have more in common with the removed, though compassionate, God of IV Ezra who can be counted on to punish all the evil people while reserving a nice place in heaven for us? Maybe we can begin to understand why some people were offended when Jesus presented the image of the shepherd as a defense of his own ministry. Read Ezekiel 34. Wouldn't you expect God to present something a little more earth-shaking as the answer to that prophetic hope? No wonder Jesus does not appear to be the messianic shepherd of Israel. His scale is too small.

STUDY QUESTIONS

1. How are Jesus' parables different from modern parables?

2. How did people in Jesus' time feel about the evil that they saw in the world around them? How do people feel about it today?

3. Why does one scholar speak of Jesus' parables as "home movies"?

4. Name at least one characteristic of the parables as told by Matthew, Mark, Luke and GTh.

5. What do you think happened to the man who found the treasure in Jesus' story? Why?

6. Give some contemporary examples of situations in which people give up prudence and security to gain something else. How does your example compare with the people in Jesus' story?

7. What do we learn about God and his people from the Lost Sheep? How might that image change the way in which we relate to others?

Chapter Two

WISDOM, PROVERB AND PARABLE

Jesus consistently reduces the scale of the great religious themes of his tradition. Instead of the nation, one meets the individual, anonymous people of daily life. Some of the parables of Jesus seem to be derived from the proverbial and folk wisdom that circulated among such people. That context is also reflected in the occupations that form the basis of the parables in the previous chapter—housewife, peasant laborer, merchant, shepherd.

Wisdom as Prudent Behavior

Much proverbial wisdom concerns itself with prudent behavior in conducting one's life—a feature that was challenged in some of Jesus' parables. Wisdom exhorts people not to be led astray by the deceits of wealth, false friendship or foolish opinions. Here are some examples from Ben Sirach:

> A man who builds his house with other people's money
> is like one who gathers stones for his burial mound.

An assembly of the wicked is like brush gathered together,
and their end is a flame of fire.
The way of sinners is smoothly paved with stones,
but its end is the pit of Hades.

(21:8–10)

The indolent may be compared to a filthy stone,
and everyone hisses at his disgrace.
The indolent may be compared to the filth of dunghills;
anyone that picks it up will shake it off his hand.

(22:1f)

One who throws a stone at birds scares them away,
and one who reviles a friend will break off the
friendship.

(22:20)

Gain the trust of your neighbor in his poverty,
that you may rejoice with him in his prosperity;
Stand by him in his time of affliction,
that you may share with him in his inheritance.

(22:23)

Some occupations are inherently likely to lead a person to sin.
Look back at the Pearl after reading this description of merchants:

A merchant can hardly keep from wrongdoing,
and a tradesman will not be declared innocent of
sin.
Many have committed sin for a trifle,
and whoever seeks to get rich will avert his eyes.
A stake is driven firmly into a fissure between two
stones,
so sin is wedged in between selling and buying.

(26:29—27:2)

Prudent, righteous conduct is presented as the best way of life in
this world. Such proverbial wisdom does not describe every sit-

uation but serves as an indication of the kind of conduct which typifies a good person.

Wisdom Traditions in the Teaching of Jesus

New Testament scholars have tended to focus on the unique in the teaching of Jesus. Therefore his use of the wisdom traditions of his people has yet to be extensively studied. One scholar finds one hundred and two such allusions in all layers of the Jesus tradition [Carlston, 1980:91]. The real number is probably larger. Proverbial material that was well known to Jesus' audience may not be familiar to us. Sometimes the form of a passage suggests that it is proverbial even though we cannot find other examples of the use of such a proverb. However, Jesus' use of wisdom materials is selective. He is not interested in forming the character of the young so that they will assume the roles set out for them by society. The advice to future leaders, the discourses on friendship, on choosing a wife and on rearing children, the warnings against greed, drunkenness and women—all are missing. Lack of such materials in Jesus' use of the wisdom tradition simply indicates that he does not appeal to it for its original purpose, the formation of future members of society.

Jesus does share with the wisdom tradition a concern for the details of everyday life. By his time, the Law and salvation history had been combined with the more secular observations of the wisdom tradition—much of Israel's wisdom tradition can be paralleled in that of other Near Eastern countries. The good life is lived with prudence and concern for the righteousness set forth in the Law. But obedience to the Law is an expression of wisdom. It is not surrounded by the complexities of scribal, technical interpretation. Similarly Jesus addresses the universal experience of humanity as the place in which one finds the truth about God's presence. One does not have to be learned in the Torah to appreciate such observations about human life.

This approach is reflected in the style of teaching employed by the wisdom tradition. Jesus uses many elements of this style. Wisdom hopes to persuade by appeal, by exhortation, and by that "telling analogy" which shows up the real folly behind certain forms of human behavior. Similarly, Jesus does not try to claim the authority of a learned interpreter of the law but to persuade by presenting his own analogies. The word "parable," *mashal,* appears as a title for two sections of Proverbs (10:1; 25:1). Nature forms many analogies in the wisdom tradition since God's presence as creator is a key element in its reflection. A parable like the Pharisee and the Publican might be recast in proverbial form: "Better to be a tax-collector who acknowledges his sin, than a Pharisee who is self-righteous before God" [so Scott:77]. Other features of Jesus' parable telling can also be related to the wisdom tradition. Visual imagery and economy of thought and line are typical. The teller states what people say; what they are thinking is left to the imagination of the audience [Scott:74]. But Jesus' parables differ from the wisdom tradition in their consistent demand that the hearer make an active effort to decide the meaning of the parable. Compare that active participation with the more passive and pessimistic use of the story of the poor wise man in Eccles 9:13-16 [Scott:80]. Wisdom teaching tells us what to think about a situation. Jesus' parables demand that we involve ourselves in making a decision about the significance of what happens.

The Challenge of Paradox

The paired parables in the previous chapter seem to use a second, simpler parable to explore the attitude presented in the first. Repeated and even contradictory sayings in the wisdom tradition perform a similar function. They sound out the complexities of life by exploring situations from different angles. The variations in Jesus' parables suggest a similar probing. Paradoxical formulations do not intend the destruction of tradition. Some parables present a structure of expected divine reward; others probe a vision of God that is perhaps too cut and dried. The wisdom tradition contains its own examples of challenge to traditional piety. Both Job and Qoheleth insist that the wise, righteous person does not always prosper. Jesus' paradoxes are somewhat different. He does not launch the radical challenge to God that we find in Job's questions (or those of IV Ezra); nor does he lapse into the worldly-wise pessimism of Qoheleth.

Instead, Jesus' challenge to the strict reward/punishment image of God seems aimed at providing room for the sinner as the one to be diligently sought out as we saw in the Lost Sheep. While we will meet many examples of the negative side of human behavior in the parables, the tone of pessimism is always missing. Jesus' vision of God and the world is one in which he rejoices. One might even suggest that Jesus is appealing to the universal elements of the wisdom tradition against themselves. Against our conventional wisdom about human life, he wishes to present a different vision. Consider the two versions of the Pharisee and the Publican, the proverb and the parable (Lk 18:9–14). One's reaction to the situation is quite different. A Pharisee could even speak the proverb as an exhortation to proper humility before God. Jesus' story makes the Pharisee look ridiculous by contrast. Though a non-Pharisee audience might be amused, a Pharisee could not adopt such a parable. The story has added just enough detail to bring off the joke/critique (depending on one's view of the principals). Those hearing the parable might respond in a variety of ways: the sinner encouraged to repent; the general audience amused; the Pharisee angered by such typecasting. Thus, there is a difference in dynamics between the universality of the proverb and the parable. The former is an observation that one might accept or reject depending on one's experience of life. The latter is a challenge designed to provoke our reaction.

Proverbial Sayings as Parables

Some parables are very close to the one-sentence proverb. They seem to have circulated independently in various versions. Since they are so short, we find them applied in various contexts. Sometimes they appear more than once in a single gospel. Some scholars prefer not to consider these sayings as parables but to reserve that category for the parables which employ narrative.

The Lamp (Mk 4:21//Mt 5:15//Lk 8:16; 11:33//GTh 24?)

The Lamp fits the two clause type of proverb in which the second clause elaborates on the first. Here are the four versions that appear in the synoptics:

Is a lamp brought in to be put under a bushel or under
a bed and not on a stand? (Mk 4:21)

No one, after lighting a lamp, covers it with a vessel, or puts it under a bed, but puts it on a stand, that those who enter may see the light. (Lk 8:16)

No one, after lighting a lamp, puts it in the cellar or under a bushel, but on a stand, that those who enter may see the light. (Lk 11:33)

Nor do men light a lamp and put it under a bushel, but on a stand, and it gives light to all in the house. (Mt 5:15)

Mark's variant seems to be independent of the Matthew/Luke type. Mt 5:15 is the simplest version of the saying and perhaps closest to the original proverb. However, he may also have changed "that those who enter may see" to "it gives light" to fit the context of the saying in the Sermon on the Mount. The disciples are being commissioned to be the light of the world (5:15). This section of Matthew adopts a motif of Jewish missionary preaching—their Law is the moral light of the world (cf Rom 2:17-24)—as an evangelical charge to Christians. What they have heard is to be the light of the world; they cannot keep it hidden away.

Mk 4:21 uses the saying to make a slightly different point about Jesus' teaching in the parables. That teaching is not some esoteric wisdom. It is to be spread abroad to be effective. Just because some have not understood or rejected it does not mean that this teaching can be shrugged off as one might do a technical article in a field one does not understand. The warnings which follow in Mark remind us that the parables call for judgment. The hearer must decide in their favor if he or she is to receive their salvation.

Lk 11:33 seems to be closest to the wisdom application of such a proverb and may reflect its original source. It is folly to put something where it is useless. Perhaps the wisdom context dealt with the uselessness of trying to reason with an ignorant, sinful or foolish person. Wisdom is useless to the fool (Sir 21:15-21). The Lukan context applies the proverb to Jesus' teaching. It is clear to anyone who is not perverse and unable to receive wisdom—as the Pharisees are (11:37ff).

This parable is mentioned in second century Gnostic lists of parables. GTh 24 gives a typically Gnostic interpretation of the parable:

> There is a light within a man of light, and it illumines the whole world. When it does not shine, there is darkness.

The parable is now understood as an allegory for the inner light of esoteric wisdom possessed by Gnostic Christians.

Garment and Wineskins
(Mk 2:21f//Mt 19:16f//Lk 5:36ff//GTh 47)

These sayings were probably used when Jesus' ministry was attacked for the violation of traditions that some understood as absolutely binding. Jesus appeals to well-known proverbs about the folly of combining the old and the new—both will be destroyed. This defense can easily be expanded to imply that Jesus is more than a reformer calling people back to the best of his tradition. His ministry presents a new initiative of God on behalf of his people. They must be ready to respond to that initiative on its own terms.

GTh 47 combines this proverb with a series of sayings about trying to serve two masters:

> It is impossible for one to ride two horses or stretch two bows. It is impossible for a servant to serve two masters; either he will honor one and despise the other.... No one drinks old wine and immediately wants to drink new. And new wine is not put in old wineskins lest they burst; and old wine is not put into a new wineskin lest it spoil it. No one sews an old patch on a new garment, because a tear will result.

Its context interprets the saying as demanding that a person decide completely for Jesus.

Salt (Mk 9:50//Mt 5:13//Lk 14:34)

Like the Lamp, this saying has two versions, Mark and

Matthew/Luke. It warns the disciples that they must testify to what they have been told in combination with the use of the Lamp as a commissioning saying in Matthew. Luke uses it to illustrate the demand that the disciple renounce all for the mission. Mk 9:50 is a different version of the saying. There the witness to be borne is that of the Christian community. "Salt" refers to the peace with one another which the disciples must show. The analogy with so vital a substance as salt suggests that such witness is not optional, not of concern only to Christians. It is a matter of crucial importance for the whole world.

Strong Man (Mk 3:27//Mt 12:29//Lk 11:21//GTh 35)

This parable is used to defend Jesus against his opponents. They claim that his exorcisms are the work of a magician (a common charge against those who claimed or were felt to have divine powers in antiquity). The proverb that only a stronger can rob a strong man is used to imply that Satan must be bound in some way for Jesus to accomplish what he does. The episode in which the proverb is set views Jesus' ministry as the defeat of Satanic power which people expected to come at the end of the world. The scale, of course, has been considerably reduced. There is no cosmic battle between Michael and Satan. Yet Jesus demonstrates the presence of the salvation that was associated with that defeat in the lives that are touched by his healing ministry.

Luke's love for story probably led him to expand the parable with v. 22—though it is possible that he knew it in a longer version. That addition makes the defeat all the more total, since the strong man's armor has been taken away. This version suggests that Jesus' ministry is not a series of temporary victories. Rather, it has permanently crippled Satan.

GTh 35 is a variant of Matthew/Mark.

Going before the Judge (Mt 5:25ff//Lk 12:58f)

Matthew and Luke have this parable in different contexts. It presupposes pagan law, since Jewish law did not imprison people for debt [Jeremias:180]. The proverb behind the parable may have been a piece of hellenistic Jewish advice on avoiding litigation: settle out of court whenever possible. That piece of conventional wisdom serves two different purposes. Matthew uses it to illustrate Jesus' teaching on anger. It teaches that a disciple will always be ready to settle a dispute. Compare the application of the Salt in Mk 9:50. Luke uses it as part of a series. The preaching of Jesus institutes a crisis to which people must respond in the same way they would if faced with the crisis of a law suit. It follows a section of proverbs about the weather which indicate that only fools would demand further signs to justify Jesus' ministry. Anyone who can tell from cloud patterns what the weather will be should be able to perceive that Jesus represents God's action on behalf of humanity. Compare his version of the Lamp in 11:33.

Proverbs in Defense of Jesus' Ministry

The previous examples of proverbs used to defend Jesus' action seem to be simple applications of existing proverbs to that particular situation. Such applications are the usual mode of using proverbs to score a point in any discussion. Other examples may have been formulated out of wisdom materials to apply more directly to that situation.

Unclean Spirit (Mt 12:43–45//Lk 11:24–26)

The saying on the return of the unclean spirit introduces an ominous note into the argument. Rejection of Jesus' message is not something to be taken lightly. Jeremias suggests that it is derived from a wisdom motif that presents relapse as a universal fact [Jeremias:197].

Children in the Market (Mt 11:16–19//Lk 7:31–35)

Both versions of this parable refer to wisdom explicitly. The original proverb was probably of the comparison type. It might have referred to the contrast between the wise and foolish. The latter are like children arguing over what to play. The parable introduces a specific subject of comparison, "this generation." The expressions "glutton and drunkard" and "friend of tax-collectors and sinners" are clearly terms of opprobrium. They were probably used to slander Jesus. The accusation "he has a demon" was also leveled at Jesus in the context of the Strong Man. Here it is attached to John the Baptist. The comparison

Fig. 6: PARALLEL VERSIONS OF
THE CHILDREN IN THE MARKET

MATTHEW	LUKE
But to what shall I compare this generation?	To what shall I compare the men of
It is like children sitting in the market places and calling to their playmates, "We piped to you and you	this generation, and what are they like?
did not dance. We wailed and you did not mourn."	They are like children sitting in the
For John came neither eating nor drinking, and	market place and calling to one another, "We piped to you and you
they say, "He has a demon."	did not dance. We wailed and you did not weep."
The Son of Man came eating and drinking, and they say,	For John the Baptist has come eating
"Behold, a glutton and a drunkard,	no bread and drinking no wine; and
a friend of tax-collectors and sinners!"	you say, "He has a demon."
Yet Wisdom is justified by her deeds.	The Son of Man has come eating and
	drinking, and you say,
	"Behold, a glutton and a drunkard,
	a friend of tax-collectors and sinners!"
	Yet Wisdom is justified by all her children.

---

turns aside such charges by reducing Jesus' opponents to the status of unruly children who spend all their time quarreling instead of playing one game or another. The use of second person, direct discourse is typical of Lukan versions of the parable. It may have been formulated to reassure those disturbed by such accusations against Jesus.

The Lukan conclusion fits the wisdom context better than Matthew's. Wisdom sayings frequently contrast the wise and foolish. The foolish, here, are the children. Now the conclusion introduces the wise, Wisdom's children. The application to John and Jesus suggests that they are true children of Wisdom. Matthew's conclusion fits several concerns of his gospel. Deeds not words are what count in the judgment. Matthew also considers Jesus himself to speak as Wisdom. Hence, his deeds are the justification required. They refer back to the deeds of Jesus mentioned in 11:2. Such Matthean Christology can be seen as a development of the way in which Jesus uses the wisdom tradition. Jesus is more than the wise men of old who prayed for the divine wisdom which made them friends of God (Wis 7:26–30). Jesus does not come simply as a wisdom teacher. Instead, he focuses that tradition on his own ministry and his call to discipleship in a renewed vision of God's presence.

Summary

Jesus' use of the wisdom tradition presents his message as part of an appeal to what we all recognize is true. This appeal does not simply confirm our collective social or cultural wisdom. Instead, what we all know appears as part of a challenge to things that we may have taken for granted. The precise nature of that challenge has to be spelled out in the larger context of Jesus' preaching. The universality of wisdom traditions provides Jesus' teaching with dimensions that are not confined to the particular theological language and symbols of first century Jews. Such discussions have the disadvantage of leaving some people out of the discussion, since they have no experience of what it means to expect messianic deliverance from the power of Satan. Students often find it very difficult to relate to the issues presented in Jewish religious texts from the time of Jesus because they do not view the world or themselves in those terms. Parables and proverbs are quite different. Everyone has an opinion about them!

STUDY QUESTIONS

1. Give an example of a proverbial saying from Israel's wisdom tradition. What values does it teach?

2. Give two examples of features in the wisdom tradition that are also found in Jesus' parable telling.

3. How does Jesus differ from the usual teacher of wisdom?

What is the relationship between Jesus and wisdom according to Matthew?

4. Give an example of a saying which has been given two different applications in the gospel tradition. How does each application relate to the theology of the evangelist in question?

5. Give an example of a parable or proverb used to answer an objection to Jesus' ministry. What is the objection? How does the proverb or parable answer that objection?

6. Why is the universality of the wisdom tradition important to the teaching of Jesus?

7. What is the role of paradox in the wisdom tradition? In the teaching of Jesus?

Chapter Three

RELIGION AND STORY

The short sayings and proverb-like parables that we have been studying show a tendency toward story. The parable is sometimes defined as "compressed story"—the shortest possible narrative unit. The parables of the Lost Sheep and the Treasure exhibit such compression. At the same time, they provoke us to go on with the tale.

Narrative and Biblical Faith

Focus on the story is not unique to Jesus. Narrative expression has special importance throughout the Bible. For Christians, it means that they are not bound to a sacred text or special language. A Christian can rehearse his or her faith anywhere by simply telling the stories that have generated that faith [Wilder, 1971:56]. Theologians have begun to turn to narrative as a mode of theological reflection. Christianity is not simply a collection of doctrines and rules. Christians must remember the stories about God and salvation as a basis for present action and for hope in the future. Such memories may be dangerous when they challenge our securities, conventions and prejudices [Metz:200–22].

Without the stories of "what happened" the special character of biblical faith would be lost. The "people of God" are those who tell and celebrate its stories as their own—whether that be the exodus from Egypt or the life, death and resurrection of Jesus of Nazareth.

Psychologists point out that what humans consider to be reality depends upon complex images that they form of the world. A new religious symbolism may change the whole image of what is real and possible for humans. The convert discovers him or herself in a new "world," the subject of a new story. This approach does not mean that Jesus' stories present the total "world view" typical of modern ideologies. They do not aim at the comprehensive account of all reality pursued by some religious sects. Jesus does call forth new vision, but the roots of his stories in the wisdom tradition show that these stories are still filled with the realism of his tradition. God appears active in the world of humans as the audience already knows them. The many applications to which a given parable or saying lends itself may even be seen as a safeguard against ideological appropriation [Crossan, 1980:22]. Another facet of the parable will challenge those who have appropriated one of its meanings to support a particular system.

The Bible as a whole is open-ended in its narrative presentation of faith. The story remains unfinished as long as the universe has not reached the perfection intended in its creation. Jesus' commission to his disciples left something real and definitely unfinished to them: they must be the light of the world. The evangelists always end the story of Jesus with this commission. Read the last chapter of any gospel. There is still a "what next?" addressed to the disciples—and, indirectly, to the reader.

The dynamics of the parables, then, reflect the open-ended character of biblical faith. Sometimes the resolution of a story involves a reversal of status or value. Frequently the parables surprise us with exaggeration or unexpected turns of plot. Their brevity often makes them a cross between riddle—"what's the solution?"—and story—"what happens next?" This combination of both rouses our expectations and leads us to attach special importance to these stories [Wilder, 1974:138–42]. At the same time, we must always recognize that the parables are stories within a larger story: the story of the gospels and, even more broadly, the story of God's dealing with his people. The open-ended character of all three levels of story challenges us to make our story part of that ongoing story.

Story and the Community of Faith

The discussion of Jesus' parable telling in Mk 4:10–12 presented something of a paradox. Jesus confronts people outside all of the religious and institutionalized authority of his time—outside the synagogue, outside the ranks of authorized teachers, outside the official text of Scripture and the technical rules for its interpretation [Crossan, 1980:16]. Yet we already see a new group of "insiders," those around Jesus. This new group is somehow "up for grabs" in the parables. It represents the context in which they are heard.

At the same time, the parables bring forward humanity itself as their horizon of meaning. They do not establish an esoteric community bound to its special talk. We have already seen hints that Jesus' refusal to be bound to socio-cultural limits had to be defended in some of the parables. Their reading of the traditional stories cannot be allowed to take charge of the possibilities for the story of faith. By bringing the parables into the story of Christians in their own times, the evangelists are also continuing the story. Metz points out that such openness to the "other" implied by Jesus' rejection of socio-cultural boundaries had to be shown in the community's willingness to be led by its own stories into a future that could not be projected in advance [195–204]. The Christian should reject all modern, secular ideologies and stories which claim to know the outcome of human history or which suppose that that outcome can be engineered with scientific precision.

Jesus' refusal to adopt a rhetoric of violence against the sinner and his imaging of a rule of God without a war of cosmic dimensions to establish it suggest important limits to Christian language about liberation. Human arrangements based on power and domination can hardly fit a view of reality which insists that the divine and hence reality itself is not conflictual. It must be possible to pursue human goals that do not require the loss of other people. Such a vision requires that the assertiveness and action necessary to the pursuit of our goals not be grounded in a picture of the individual as a private, independent center of power but in the purposes of God and humanity's relationship to him [Lynch:196–208]. The stories of Jesus might even be said to be "outside Christianity" if what is really at stake is the story of all of us—not just that of some Galileans living under Roman rule, not just of pagans finding a new vision of God, not even just the story of Christian communities charged with mediating that story to humanity in the concrete situations of the world.

Approaching the Parable as Story

The new interest in biblical narrative has led to many attempts to apply the various methods of literary criticism to its stories. We can hardly survey them all; nor would we claim that literary analysis alone can provide the key to biblical meanings. But its techniques can improve our reading of the text by helping us slow down and appreciate the construction of some very simple and familiar stories. Different approaches highlight different elements in the parables. When we compare one interpretation with another we begin to appreciate the multi-dimensional meaning of the parables. In this chapter we will introduce some common forms of literary analysis being used in parables research. They will all be combined in the "literary analysis" section of subsequent discussions of individual parables.

Rhetorical Criticism

Rhetorical criticism calls our attention to the parable as a literary creation. We must pay careful attention to how words are used. What words and phrases are repeated in the text? Are they repeated in parallel (a,b,a',b') patterns or chiastic (a,b,b',a') ones? Words and phrases that are nearly identical are used for this type of analysis. Themes are not used, since they are too often subject to the overall understanding of a particular interpreter. Thematic analyses may foreclose certain meanings implied in a particular parable.

Careful attention must be paid to divisions within a story. Introductory and concluding phrases may indicate various sections. Characters enter and exit. Other divisions are marked off when the story shifts from narrated, third person, discourse (ND) to direct, second person, discourse (DD). Narrated discourse can be introduced to highlight a point or it can be used to introduce the circumstances of a parable and to slide over elements that might distract from the focus of the story. Both the shifts in the manner of discourse and the amount of time and detailed verbal structure highlight particular sections of parables. The longest and most elaborately designed sections capture our attention and are crucial to the impression left by the story as a whole [Tolbert, 1979:74–91].

When looking at a story, we also must ask what actions are involved in the story. Those with more than one action follow two patterns. In some, the first is over before the second begins. The two actions may comment on each other. Often the sections will be parallel halves with similar rhetorical structure. Others are concentric. The first begins, is interrupted by the second, then concludes. This chiastic type often contains parallel repetitions in the central part of the story. These techniques of rhetorical analysis ask us to pay careful attention to the overall design of a parable.

Plot Analysis

Concern for "what happens" in a parable leads to various types of plot analysis. The simplest [Via, 1973] classifies plots as comic or tragic. The low mimetic mode of the parable distinguishes such categories from those typical of the classical dramatists. In the parable, the key is how the central character ends up. Has he or she received a lucky break where none would have been expected (comic)? Or has unexpected disaster overtaken him or her (tragic)?

Slightly more complex plot analysis is possible in parables which have three principals [Funk, 1974a]. Only two of the possible relationships are developed in a given parable. In one type, a figure, the Determiner (D), sets the stage. The other two characters (R1, R2) respond. Their responses may be narrated in sequence or interlocked in chiastic fashion. Very often one response will lead to a tragic outcome, the other to a comic one. The pattern of relationships is different in the second group. The plot turns on the D-R1 relationship. The third character (r) simply advances the relationship between the first two—often because D has vanished from the story for a while. When the plots are concentric, one finds a sequence: action/crisis/resolution. When they are parallel: crisis/response 1/response 2. The second type usually involves a double reversal of fortune for R1 and goes crisis/response/resolution.

Plot analysis leads to another question about the outcome of the story. Sometimes one expects the outcome. It represents the conventional wisdom about what such characters deserve. But in other cases, as we saw with the Lost Sheep and the Treasure, the outcome is unexpected. Many interpreters argue that most parables involve some reversal of expectation. The parable intends to overturn some cherished or taken-for-granted assumptions about the world which are blocking the hearer's ability to discern the action of God.

Structuralist Analysis

Russian and French structuralists analyze narrative in abstract, formal categories derived from folklore. They claim to indicate the meaning lodged in preconceptual operations of the mind. Certain elements of their study of folklore can be used to help us locate semantic ambiguities in the parables of Jesus. Every story requires three pairs of opposed roles. Called actants, they form a basic lexicon of elements in a narrative.

(1) *Subject/Object:* They represent the axis of the story. The Subject's role is defined over against the Object, which is the focus of his/her concern.

(2) *Sender/Receiver:* The Receiver may be the Subject if the Object of the story is personal well-being rather than a solution to another's pressing problem. However, the story usually gets off the ground when someone or something, the Sender, alerts the Subject to the Receiver's need for the Object.

(3) *Helper/Adversary:* The story presumes that the Subject cannot carry out a task simply. Otherwise, those before him or her would have done so. He or she must usually begin by acquiring the necessary Helper—human assistant, special weapon, protective charm, hidden knowledge, divine favor or whatever. Similarly, the quest is hindered by various Adversaries, which are usually correlated with the type of Helper required.

These roles are often arranged in what is called an actant diagram:

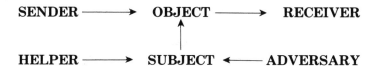

Difficulties in interpreting a story may arise because one or another role is not clearly indicated.

A long story lends itself to analysis of various plots and subplots during which the actants may change. The narrative action falls into various units called syntagms: (1) performative—the actions the subject either performs or fails to in completing the tasks before him or her; (2) contractual—the subject must agree to undertake the necessary mission in the first place (and in various subplots along the way); (3) disjunctional (departure/return)—the subject must usually depart and later return to his or her usual home and relationships. Parables are usually too short to make syntagmatic analysis valuable.

The Prodigal Son (Lk 15:11–32)

The Prodigal Son exemplifies all of the features that we have been describing. Its title is somewhat deceptive, since the parable involves both sons. It concludes with two parallel confrontations between father and son.

The story plays on a well-known folk story: the younger son who leaves home to seek his fortune. Relationships between elder and younger brothers have been explored in Old Testament stories such as Esau and Jacob and Joseph and his brothers. Usually, younger sons are tested by a period of hardship: years of labor for his father-in-law in Jacob's case, slavery and imprisonment in Joseph's. Only after that testing do they advance to prosperity. The conclusion of such tales requires that the prosperity and superiority of the younger son be revealed to his elder brother(s) and sometimes also to his father. The Prodigal Son invokes motifs from the Joseph story—the clothes, the ring, the banquet.

This boy is no Joseph. Joseph is imprisoned on a false charge of sexual misconduct. The Prodigal wastes his inheritance in such misconduct. He then becomes a swineherd, an occupation which excluded a Jew from being a member of the people of God. He is subject to destitution and famine. He does not rescue the country and his family from it as Joseph does. This boy is almost a parody of the Joseph/Jacob type.

Legal evidence shows that the initial division of property was possible. It was not an act of disrespect for the father. The father did not have to consent. Since he agrees, one assumes that he found nothing objectionable in the arrangement. He would remain in control of the farm for life but could no longer sell without the elder son's consent. Having taken his inheritance, the younger son has no further claims on the property. Jesus' audience would probably not have seen the introduction as anything more than a way of getting the story going.

Rhetorical Analysis

The actions and modes of discourse may be outlined as follows:

    I.   Introduction (v. 11; ND).
   II.   Younger son initiates division of property (v. 12; DD)
  III.   Younger in far country (vv. 13–16; ND)
        a. his squandering (v. 13)
        b. his famine (vv. 14–16)

These opening sections, predominately in narrated discourse, may be said to set the scene for the real focus of the story, the return, which is marked by the shift to direct discourse as the younger son "comes to himself."

   IV.   Younger comes to himself (vv. 17–19; DD)
    V.   Father's greeting (vv. 20–24; ND—DD—ND)
        a. meeting (v. 20; ND)
        b. son to father, repentance (v. 21; DD)
        c. father to servants: prepare feast (vv. 22–24a; DD)
        d. conclusion (v. 24b; ND)
   VI.   Father seeks elder son (vv. 25–32; ND—DD)
        a. elder son in the fields (v. 25; ND)

b. elder son to servant (vv. 26–27a; DD)
c. father to elder son (vv. 27a–32; DD)

Verse 32 repeats the conclusion to the meeting of the father and the younger son in v. 24. Further parallels between the episodes can be adduced:

(1) Both are "in the field(s)."
(2) Having decided to return, the younger is met by the father "while he was yet at a distance." The elder "came and drew near" when he inquires about the situation and decides not to go in.
(3) Hunger brings the younger to his senses; the sounds of the feast provoke the inquiry and anger of the elder.
(4) The father comes out after both sons.

The squandered property (v. 13) is an anti-type of the feasting and merry-making that ties the second half together (vv. 23, 24, 26, 29, 32). The younger's squandered property might also be contrasted with the "saved property" of the elder who has never had such a feast with his friends. All these images of abundant food form a sharp contrast with the famine which motivates the action of the central section. The father's explanation of his action correlates these contrasts with that of death and life.

The father-younger son section is most elaborate, since it establishes a new perception of the father which comes as a surprise to both sons. The younger agrees with the elder that all he deserves is the status of servant. Instead, he is treated to a welcome appropriate to the return of a successful younger son. Notice that the story does not emphasize the emotions of the father. He does not even respond to the younger son but gives orders to the servants. He has already welcomed the younger son before the latter gives his speech. Dialogue with the elder is required, since the father must answer the accusation made by the elder son.

Plot Analysis

The rhetorical complexities of the story are mirrored in the plot. The basic structure of such stories was familiar to the audience. Their plot requires that the younger find himself in some sort of adversity. The entertainment of the story would lie in seeing how the younger son managed to get himself out of the initial scrape. The audience would expect an upturn in the young man's fortunes. But he does not turn out to be any folktale younger son. All he does is return home hoping that his father will bail him out. Sure enough, his good luck is located back home in the person of his father. The elder son's reaction probably mirrors that of many in the audience. The younger is not even scolded for his behavior. Instead, he receives a welcome all out of proportion to what he deserves.

Though the plot is clearly "comic" as far as the younger son is concerned, the situation of the elder is not as clear. Many interpretations assume that he remained impervious to the father's plea. His anger kept him from going in. A variant on this "tragic" reading holds that the father is the one who suffers unexpected reversal. His extravagance toward a profligate but favored younger son has poisoned his relationship with the elder [Breech:34]. We are never told how the story ended. The endings that different people supply often say a great deal about their image of family relationships. Some assume he stays out. Others think that he goes in out of obedience but does not join in the festivity. Still others feel that the joyousness of the occasion and his love for his father will overcome his anger, and that he will eventually participate.

There is just as much disagreement over the actant roles in this story. Folklore traditions would make the subject the younger son. Others suggest that the father is the real subject of this story, since he is the one who must react appropriately to the situations created by each of his two sons. The issue presented is whether or not the father is successful in reconciling both sons by the end of the story. In that case the plot remains unfinished. The hearer must decide whether its outcome is tragic or comic.

Structuralist Analysis

Such ambiguity as to subject is not at all uncommon. The subject often appears as a passive figure who must respond to situations created by others [Scholes:110]. Treated as a folktale of the younger son, the surprising thing about this parable is his failure to surmount adversity and return home wealthier than his elder brother. Yet the tragedy is somewhat reversed when the father treats him as a successful younger son anyway. The actant diagram for this portion of the story might be:

SOCIAL/LEGAL→WEALTH ——————→ SELF AND FAMILY
CONVENTION

HIS SHARE OF ——→ SON ←—————— CHARACTER/FAMINE
ESTATE FATHER

However, the story does not end with the reception of the younger son. (For arguments against scholars who think that it does, see Carlston, 1975b.) The father's action is the focus of the second half of the story. He wishes to have both sons included in the rejoicing. He reminds the elder son that the legal relationship between them can never be broken. The elder already has title to all that the father owns. Ambiguity arises in this part of the story because we do not know whether the elder went in or not. The father must overcome the sources of the elder son's anger: social and moral conventions that seem to be violated in the father's treatment of the younger; the resentment which stems from seeing the profligate apparently rewarded, while he has been working almost like the servant that the younger thought he would become and never been rewarded. The father makes two appeals. First, he points to the unbreakable legal relationship between himself and the elder son. Second, he appeals to the joy that should characterize such an occasion. An actant diagram might look something like this:

LOVE FOR ——————→ RECONCILIATION ——————→ BROTHERS
BOTH SONS

LEGAL BOND ——————→ FATHER ←——HIS TREATMENT
JOY   OF YOUNGER
                                   ANGER
                                   RESENTMENT

The parallel endings to both sections focus on joy as the primary motivation for the father's behavior and for that behavior he hopes the elder son will adopt. The very extravagance of the welcome may catch the audience unaware so that they agree with the father in finding the elder son's behavior petty and unreasonable. Yet his anger and resentment could also be seen as the other side of those very virtues which are typical of a good elder son—obedience to his father and devotion to his duties.

The context of the parable in Luke provides another actant diagram which may be said to underlie the ambiguities inherent in the story. Jesus is faced with hostile Pharisees. The Christian reader knows that he will not succeed in reconciling them to his proclamation of forgiveness for sinners. But at this point in the narrative that question is still open. An actant diagram for the larger context might be:

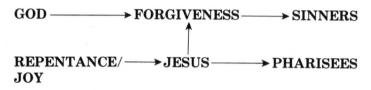

In the larger narrative the parable itself might be cast as Helper. The father acknowledges the legitimacy of the elder son's claim but not the appropriateness of his response in the particular situation. If the parable succeeds, Jesus will have turned aside the anger of his critics and enabled them to share in the joy of the kingdom of God.

Psychological Interpretations

A story so concerned with the dynamics of love and anger within the family lends itself to a variety of psychological interpretations. Some take the characters as symbols for the tensions that are part of every individual psyche.

A Jungian approach to the story sees it as representing the necessary integration of the shadow side of the personality, usually manifest in emotions, prejudices and other negative behavior, into the ego so that these elements will no longer run our life from the unconscious [Via, 1975]. Both sons represent negative elements which must be made conscious and integrated into the personality. The younger represents all tendencies to live without convention and to follow the lead of one's instincts. Gentiles, swine, and sexual immorality all combined as a powerful symbol for the instinctual behavior that was totally opposed to God in the Jewish psyche. But the righteousness of the dutiful elder son also has a negative side. It spawns anger and resentment.

The negative side of the younger son's behavior requires repentance. He recognizes the values represented by his brother and is even willing to undertake the renunciation that would be required to be a servant in his father's household—better than starving to death as a swineherd for a Gentile! The joyous conclusion comes when the return home does not require such a renunciation on his part. The rigid obedience and moralism of the elder might be said to have led him to a similar position. He seems to perceive himself more as a servant than as the legally favored son. The father's intervention, a representation of the Spirit archetype as is the younger son's "coming to himself," must transform the negative side of such obedience. This transformation does not condemn the elder son (though commentators often do so) but calls him to participate in the celebration. The obedient moralist must be able to step beyond that into the joy of the feast—without prejudice to his obedience.

Jesus could be said to have created the parable as an image of the transformations required in the audience. The shadow side of rigid obedience to the Law—which is secretly resentful of the profligate behavior of sinners—cannot share the joy of forgiveness and repentance without becoming conscious of how inappropriate it is to the present context. This parable might even be said to give us a glimpse of the consciousness of God that enabled Jesus to carry out the ministry he did and to avoid the rhetoric of apocalyptic judgment—a cosmic expression of the resentment of the righteous. It suggests that his disciples had to go through a similar process of transformation if they were to perceive the depths of his message. Otherwise they might trivialize it as a license to ditch all restraint and morality. Both Matthew and Paul had to confront Christians whose immaturity had led them to make such a mistake.

Freudian interpretations, grounded in a conviction that the structure of the psyche was set during the biological process of evolution [Sulloway:365–444], lack the dimensions of spiritual transformation implied in the Jungian context. They may focus either on relationships within elements of the psyche or on the ambivalence of father-son and brother-brother relationships within the family [Tolbert, 1975:209–215; 1979:104f].

The three characters may be identified with three elements of the psyche. The younger son represents the unrestrained, instinctual drives, the Id. The elder represents the equally unrestrained demands of tradition and morality internalized as Superego. His anger reflects the internalized aggression that attends the formation of conscience and is expressed in the severity of moral demand. The father stands in the place of the Ego, which must mediate. Unrestrained instinctual behavior cannot be condoned; yet the strict demands of the Superego must be relaxed so that the person can participate in the instinctual pleasures of the banquet. Thus the story becomes an illustration of the mediation required in any healthy adult personality. The Ego must negotiate between instinct and pleasure, on the one hand, and duty or societal obligation on the other.

Application of Freudian approaches to the dynamics of family relationships raises questions about the father's behavior [Tolbert, 1979:108–110]. His extravagant reception may represent over-compensation for his real feelings of anger and hostility toward his son. The elder projects his hostility toward his brother onto the father when accusing him of never having provided him with a feast. This reading makes the younger son the focus of the ambivalent feelings of love and hate felt by the other characters. It brings out the importance of the younger son in determining reactions throughout the story. But it does not seem to offer an adequate picture of the father's discussion with the elder. The father acknowledges some justice to the son's reaction, but he still insists on reconciliation and the appropriateness of his response. Such a position does not appear to represent veiled hostility.

First century hearers would not have expressed their perception of the story in psychological terms. However, the analysis suggested by twentieth century critics does provide insight into the human dynamics underlying such stories. It also indicates to us the challenges presented to a person by the message of Jesus. These challenges may require transformation or reorganization of the foundational processes of the psyche.

Community Reconciliation

The Lukan context suggests that the parable may also be viewed in anthropological terms as a "social drama" [Turner:78f]. Communities use ritual and its attendant stories to moderate situations of internal tension. Jesus has been presenting God as more than one who receives repentant sinners. His contemporaries would have agreed with that. He has presented God as actively searching out the sinner and outcast. Further, he seems to have enacted this inclusive concern in the actual community between himself, his disciples and sinners—without waiting for them to have gone through rituals of repentance that would have restored them to the community of the righteous. The strains of such a community may well have shown themselves among his followers. Criticism by outsiders such as the Pharisees could well have increased that tension. Perhaps Jesus is wrong.

Rather than focus on the Pharisees as exemplars of righteousness as Luke does, we could suggest that what is at stake is the "Pharisee" within the community around Jesus. The story must mediate reconciliation of the tensions created by their feelings. It succeeds if its expression of those feelings also makes them seem trivial, if the disciples feel that the elder should go in and rejoice and hence are willing to do so themselves. Then they will not be put off by elements of extravagance in Jesus' ministry or the resonance that others' criticism may have with some of their own feelings. After all, the disciples no less than outsiders must come to share the joy of Jesus' vision. The story acknowledges a certain felt inequality between the righteous and the sinner, but it insists that both can come to participate in the same feast. In order to do so, the story cannot simply be an allegory for God. The father's behavior must represent a real human possibility. Otherwise, one could allow such forgiveness to God, who is different anyway, and not require it in the community. But we can all think of human examples of such fathers, such younger and elder sons. This story is more extravagant and something of an affront to the conventional values of younger son tales, but it is nonetheless real. Hence the logic of such a story: "If this can be the case with fathers and sons, how much the more with God."

Notice that this story does not require everyone to identify with the sinfulness of the younger son and his experience of forgiveness. Some are righteous, after all. The test for them is whether or not they can take the same joy in the younger son that the father does. The story stands not simply as an example for individuals but as a challenge to the community of disciples. Can they exhibit such reconciliation?

Man with Two Sons (Mt 21:28–31a)

This parable, which is little more than an expanded proverb, explores the simpler pattern of repentance. The proverbial background is evident: Better the son who repents and obeys his father than the son who promises obedience but does not. Matthew adds a Q saying (vv. 31b–32//Lk 7:29f) about the tax-collectors and harlots getting into the kingdom ahead of the righteous because they repented at the preaching of John the Baptist. What a person does counts, not what he or she promises. The audience might have been reminded of the prophets warning Israel that her prayers and sacrifices were nothing without deeds of justice and mercy. Matthew uses this parable against Pharisaic criticism of Jesus. It might originally have been part of Jesus' call to repentance and renewed obedience to the intention of God behind the Law.

Summary

Both stories indicate what it meant for Jesus to seek to win all, righteous and sinners, for the rule of God. The dichotomizing tendencies of human judgments must be overcome. So must the folktales of successful younger sons. Neither son is allowed to win at the expense of the other. Perhaps such a story seems "unheroic" in contrast to the more common stories that might inspire younger sons to venture forth as they must with confidence. Yet its image is closer to reality for that. Both are sons like those we all know. Our own life, not a tale, provides possibilities and models for divine and community action.

STUDY QUESTIONS

1. Why is story-telling fundamental to biblical faith?

2. What is the relationship between stories and the community of faith?

3. Give three examples of questions that a rhetorical analysis of a parable must answer.

4. Which character would you consider to be the Determiner in the Prodigal Son? Why?

5. Do you think that the plot of the Prodigal Son is tragic or comic? Why?

6. Describe the three pairs of relationships in the actant diagram using examples from the Prodigal Son.

7. How might relationships in your family or your community be different if the Prodigal Son story were a model for relationships between people?

8. Which character in the Prodigal Son best fits your reactions and feelings? How does the story suggest that you change?

Chapter Four

HINTS FOR READING PARABLES

The Prodigal Son shows that a parable can deliver a series of meanings. It can speak about different aspects of reality at one time. This variety does not mean that any meaning fits the story, however. Before continuing with a study of specific issues that arise in connection with Jesus' parables, we should pause to review some of the basic elements of parable interpretation. What are the different questions that we put to a parable as we study it?

Text Questions

(1) *What text* is being interpreted? Is it a reconstruction from the various versions? Is it that of one evangelist? Does it include the context of the parable in the gospel? Are there any obvious additions to the story by the evangelist?

(2) *Read the text.* Focus your reading by applying methods of literary analysis. Map out the relationships in the story. Look for points that seem to be exaggerated or ambiguous. If you are reading someone else's interpretation, check his or her description of the relationships, exaggerations and ambiguities against

yours. Does the interpretation given deal with all the points involved or only some of them? Does it consider some features to be unimportant because the overall structure of the story de-emphasizes them?

Context Questions

(1) The *theoretical context* behind a given interpretation should not be overlooked. Historians, literary critics, anthropologists, psychologists, philosophers and theologians are all looking for different aspects of reality in approaching a story. You may need more information about a particular method in order to decide if it is properly applied to the parable in question.

(2) *Gospel context* plays an important role in specifying the meaning of particular parables. Different evangelists pick up different elements in the story. Outline the section in which the parable occurs. How does surrounding material relate to the themes of the parable? Are there other themes typical of the evangelist in question that illuminate his interpretation of the story?

(3) *Historical context* tries to situate the parable in the teaching and ministry of Jesus. Sometimes other sayings of Jesus or situations which seem to have been typical of his ministry help us suggest an appropriate setting. In other cases, interpreters can only make what seems to be a "good guess" based on their overall feeling for the ministry of Jesus. We also need information about life in first century Palestine—legal arrangements, social customs, political and economic realities, as well as the "hot topics" of religious concern. At some points we have fairly good historical and archaeological evidence; at others, we may only be able to guess the situation from what we know of contemporary village life or that in other countries of the first century. Such careful study of historical context helps us avoid modernizing a story by injecting our own cultural values back into a different world.

Meaning Questions

Often when people ask what a parable "means" they are not interested in the type of meaning sought by the historian: What would the original audience have said it meant if we could have asked them? Or: What do the evangelists show the parable to have meant in the early Christian communities? They are asking whether or not the parable has any significance for their lives today. Can we learn anything of value from it?

(1) *Human significance* may be found in insights that seem to apply to any human person, for example, the psychological dimensions of the story of the Prodigal Son. Its picture of interpersonal dynamics does not seem bound to the cultural milieu of the first century Middle East. We have also seen that the elements of wisdom tradition and folklore in the parables of Jesus contribute to such a universal scope. Inheritance and occupational patterns do not require the younger sons of our society to go off the family farm and the elder to stay home and begin to assume responsibility as head of the family, but we see the dynamics of elder/younger in our own families. The anger or resentment of the "dutiful" in the face of a more prodigal but seemingly favored sibling may be all the more confused because there are no socially established roles and rewards that children grow up knowing they will fit into. How do we handle reconciliation in such cases? Are we sensitive to the child who is "no problem"? Can we make family life a zero-sum game in which all are winners? One person does not succeed at the expense and sacrifice of others in the family.

(2) *Religious significance* for the present is embodied in the preservation of the parables as teaching by the community of believers. They are part of a Sacred Scripture which claims to be more than an ad hoc record of the founder's attempts to persuade others to follow him—more, even, than wise insight into humans and their behavior. It claims to embody a message of salvation that people can neglect only to their own detriment. The Prodigal Son hints that that salvation is not a contest for a few winners to rejoice in their victory at the expense of a lot of losers. Rather, it is the kind of game in which every effort is made to help each player hit a home run. All are to experience the "thrill of victory" and leave the agony of defeat to ABC Sports.

This image is particularly important for the religious community that Jesus envisages among his disciples. The dynamics of righteousness can often be hostile to outsiders, to sinners, and even to those who are making their own steps back to God. A student now working his way back to Catholicism after a stint with a fundamentalist group expressed his feelings this way: "You know, they were all such good Christians, but something about it was like having a big stone in my gut. Maybe it's just that I could never be as good as they were." Maybe. Maybe it's just that they could only feel their righteousness by passing negative judgments on others as the elder son does with regard to his younger brother. In any case, a community based on Jesus' vision can never allow such dynamics to take hold.

Steps You Can Take

Let's summarize the steps you can take in working out an interpretation of a parable for yourself.

(1) Pick out the text to be interpreted and study it. Use some of the methods of literary analysis. What happens? How is the story put together? Are there different versions?

(2) Look in a commentary on the gospel in question or a book on the parables of Jesus to find any historical background to the story. Also look for Old Testament allusions and other stories on a related theme.

(3) The same sources should suggest aspects of Jesus' teaching or ministry that might be reflected in this parable. Cross references to other passages in your Bible may also be of help.

(4) What are the human dimensions of the story? Can you think of other examples of the kind of interaction represented? What aspects of human relationships are valued according to the story? Which ones is the story suggesting that we change or view in a different light?

(5) What meaning does the parable have for Christians? The use of the parable by the evangelists often gives us indications of how they used the parable in their own preaching. How will Christians relate to one another and to God if they take the parable seriously?

Rich Man and Lazarus (Lk 16:19–31)

The Rich Man and Lazarus is another finely crafted narrative, divided into several scenes. The fate of the poor man sets the stage for the actions of the rich, his neglect of the poor during his earthly life and his failure to win assistance in the after-life.

Literary Analysis

The parable is carefully divided into sections.

I. Two Contrasting Fates (vv. 19–21; ND)

	RICH MAN	LAZARUS
a)	in life:	
	inside	at the gate
	clothed in purple, fine linen	covered with sores
	feasted sumptuously every day	so hungry desired to eat crumbs [like a dog]
		is licked [feasted on] by dogs
b)	in death:	
	died	died
	was buried	carried by angels to Abraham's bosom

II. Rich Man's attempt to get help from Abraham through the sending of Lazarus (vv. 24–31; DD):

a) to him to quench his thirst

 i. answer summarizing the first part:

	RICH MAN	LAZARUS
in life:		
	good things	evil
in death:		
	torment	comfort

 ii. answer reversing the geography of life and death: there is an unbridgeable gulf no one can cross. (Contrast, life in which Lazarus lay at the door of the man's house. The man passed by him daily.)

b) to his brothers to prevent their coming to torment

 i. answer: Moses and the prophets.

 ii. objection: someone from the dead and they will repent.

 iii. answer: not if they do not heed Moses and the prophets.

The plot of the story reverses the fate of the rich and poor man. Jeremias points to a rabbinic adaptation of an Egyptian folktale. A rich tax-collector is tormented in Hades while a poor scholar is in a paradise watered by flowing streams [183]. As a variant of that type of story, the actant diagram would be:

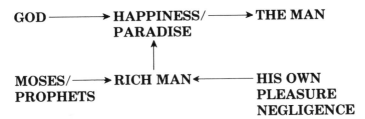

The rich man has lost salvation because his own self-indulgence made him blind to God's command to care for the poor even with a clear example of such need lying on his doorstep.

When we compare this story with the rabbinic version, we notice that it is not as heavily moralized. The rich man is negligent but not engaged in an occupation recognized as evil such as tax-collecting. The poor man is rewarded simply for his suffering, not because he has also been a pious student of the Law. The major emphasis in the story does not fall on the reversal as much as on the ensuing dialogue between the rich man and Abraham. Sinners do not usually get such a lengthy hearing. This man is almost comical in his persistence. When he sees the reversal of fates, he does not acknowledge his own guilt but tries to get relief from Lazarus—even though he had never given him any. The repeated rejection of his pleas by reference to Moses and the prophets shows that disregard for them was typical of this man's life. His appeal for extra aid to his brothers acknowledges the fact that they are not likely to hear Moses and the prophets either.

Historical Background

Striking parallels to the imagery of this parable come from Enoch traditions widely circulated in the time of Jesus. These writings claimed to record the heavenly journeys of the mysterious Enoch, journeys on which he saw the fate of the wicked. They are usually punished in fiery chasms such as we find here.

1 Enoch contains sections of woes against the rich for their persecution of the righteous poor. Angels serve as guardians of the
poor. 1 Enoch also contains scenes of judgment in which the rich
recognize and lament the punishment that their life has de-
served. Here are some examples of its preaching:

> Woe to you who devour the finest wheat, and drink wine
> in large bowls, and trample the lowly with your might.
> (96:5)

> Woe to you who acquire silver and gold unrighteously
> and say, "We have acquired riches and possessions; we
> have acquired everything we wanted. Now let's do what
> we intended, for we have collected silver; we have many
> farmers in our houses; our granaries are full to the brim
> as with water." Yes, like water your lies shall flow
> away. Your riches will not last but will fly away from
> you, for you have acquired it all in unrighteousness. You
> will be handed over to a great curse. (97:8–10)

> Now I swear to you, the righteous, by the glory of the
> Great, Honored and Mighty One in his rule and by his
> greatness, I swear. I know a mystery. I have read the
> heavenly tablets and seen the holy books and found
> written concerning them (the righteous): All goodness
> and joy are prepared for them, and are written down for
> the spirits who have died in righteousness. Manifold
> good shall be given to you in recompense for your labors,
> and your lot is abundantly beyond the lot of the living.
> The spirits of those who have died in righteousness shall
> live and rejoice. Their spirits shall not perish, nor their
> memory from the presence of the Great One unto all
> generations. Therefore, no longer fear their (the wick-
> ed's) perversity. Woe to you sinners, when you have
> died. If you die in the wealth of your sins, and those like
> you say, "Blessed are the sinners. They have lived a long
> life. Now they have died in prosperity and wealth. They
> did not suffer tribulation or murder in life, and they
> have died in honor. Judgment was not executed on them
> during their life," know that their souls will be sent
> down into Sheol, and they will be wretched in their

great tribulation. Your spirits will enter darkness and chains and a burning flame where there is terrible judgment; and the great judgment shall be for all the generations of the world. Woe to you for you will have no peace. (103:1–8)

The rich man in the parable is rather typical of the picture of the rich in this preaching. 1 Enoch suggests that their lack of concern for Moses and the prophets was based on the prosperity and happiness of their earthly life. The rich were confident that all was well if things were going well in their earthly life. No wonder the rich man thinks that his brothers require some other warning. He admits that they do not listen to the word of God in Moses and the prophets. At the same time, Jesus' story is much less grand in scale when it comes to portraying the sinner in hell. He is almost pathetic in his attempts to bargain with Abraham across the fiery abyss.

Teaching of Jesus

Both the comic scale of the parable and its lack of vindictiveness toward the rich are typical of Jesus' parables. While 1 Enoch comes very close to making the rich as such the object of damnation, Jesus' parable still leaves room for their conversion. Luke is very much concerned with instructing wealthy Christians in the duties of almsgiving. Early Christians did not condemn wealth as such. However, it can create a false security which makes the individual impervious to the call of salvation, or, as in the story of the rich young man (Mk 10:17–31 par), unable to heed the call to discipleship.

Human Significance

The peculiar ending of this parable contributes to its human significance. The story is not a projection of the fantasies and hostilities of the poor as some accuse the judgment scenes and woes in 1 Enoch of being. Lazarus does not exult over the torment suffered by the rich man as an exalted Israel does over its enemies in other Jewish apocalypses. Instead, the rich man is pictured as one who still does not grasp his situation. He is not wailing and lamenting like a proper sinner but trying to get out of the situation by bargaining with Abraham. Such disregard has its modern analogies. *The New York Times* carried a story of a suit being brought by the daughter-in-law of the Wrigley chewing gum heiress against the estate to recover inheritance that she feels unduly deprived of. Her mother-in-law had disinherited her when she heard her say of $1,000 worth of underwear that she had brought home without trying on for size, "If it doesn't fit, I'll throw it out and buy more." Regardless of the merits of the suit, this story is an example of the complete wastefulness and disregard typical of certain rich people. Jesus' parable suggests that such people may even come to the point that they cannot recognize their true situation when they are frying in hell!

The rich man is rather pathetic. Jesus does not encourage the righteous by promising salvation and then describing the tortures awaiting sinners as in the third 1 Enoch passage. He simply paints us a picture of such a rich person. The picture raises a question: Would you like to be such a person? Some people still say that they would and let the future take care of itself. Their response reminds us that the parables are not out to force particular values on the audience—contrast 1 Enoch. This parable makes it clear enough that Lazarus is preferred to the rich man. It also points out that the person who chooses to be like the rich man may be a rather pathetic figure indeed.

Religious Significance

Jesus' audience was familiar with the teaching of the Law and the prophets. They were probably also familiar with the kind of preaching embodied in the Enoch traditions. They knew that wealth could blind a person to the obligations of justice and concern for the poor. They knew that those who pursued wealth often did so by deliberately oppressing others. The Gentile Christians for whom Luke wrote, on the other hand, did not have such a heritage. Generosity was practiced only toward those of one's own class, those who could pay you back. Therefore, Luke emphasizes a number of parables which deal with the obligation to aid the poor. We still find Christians needing to be reminded that the idol of material prosperity can be a dangerous one. It may blind us to more serious issues of justice.

Rich Fool (Lk 12:16–21//GTh 63)

Compare this parable with the words of the rich in the second Enoch passage. The rich man thinks that he will be able to sit back and enjoy his immense wealth. Instead, he dies that night. GTh 63 appears to be an abbreviated version of the story:

> There was a rich man with a lot of money. He said, "I will put my money to use so that I may sow and reap and fill my storehouse with produce; then I will lack nothing." Those were his intentions, but that very night he died.

Some changes are typical of GTh. The man is no longer a rich farmer as in Luke and 1 Enoch, but someone looking for an investment. GTh typically supposes such a context of business and trade rather than the village agricultural scale of the parables.

Luke's version is so close to 1 Enoch that some think it may have been based on Enoch traditions. However, a similar description appears in the wisdom tradition:

> There is a man who is rich through his diligence and self-denial, and this is the reward allotted to him when he says, "I have found rest, and now I shall enjoy my goods!": he does not know how much time will pass until he leaves them to others. Stand by your task; attend to it, and grow old in your work. (Sir 11:18–20)

Both Luke and 1 Enoch may have expanded a common wisdom observation. Riches never provide the secure life that they promise, since death can intervene at any moment. Lk 12:21 exhorts Christians to gain wealth before God—presumably by giving their excess to the poor rather than building bigger and better grain elevators.

The structure of the parable is not complex:

  I. Situation (v. 16; ND)
 II. Rich man's plans (vv. 17–19; DD)
III. God's judgment (v. 20; DD)

The dialogue makes this parable more dramatic than 1 Enoch or Sirach. The sharp incisive judgment which concludes the parable forms a striking contrast to the rich man's deliberations. There is also an element of exaggeration that makes the parable comic in contrast with the other versions of such preaching. The man plans to pull down all the barns in order to build bigger ones. That passage always puzzled me as a child, since I could not figure out what the man would do with everything in the old barns while he was building the new ones. Of course, it does make the man appear as foolish as the story says.

The type of wisdom preaching which underlies this parable was common in early Christianity. Look at the description of the calculations of merchants in Jas 4:13–17. He follows the passage with woes similar to what we find in the Enoch tradition. The parable, on the other hand, lacks further reference to the man's fate. The short sentence of judgment is sufficient for the audience to supply that.

Luke has combined the parable with a story in which Jesus is asked to settle an inheritance dispute (vv. 13–15) and followed it with sayings against anxiety over material well-being (vv. 22–34). The final sayings of the section (vv. 33f) instruct Christians to gain possessions that really count by giving generously to the poor. Thus, the whole unit provides extended instruction on the proper and improper attitude toward wealth. The disciple can never fall into the trap of thinking that his or her life is constituted by possessions.

Summary

These parables are typical of the almost comic mode in which the parables present their vision. This tone is quite different from the educational advice of Sirach and from the thundering preaching of 1 Enoch, though much of what those traditions say about the rich is reflected in these parables. But Jesus approaches the question by holding up small-scale images that ask his audience to scrutinize the attitudes of such people. The audience is not invited to feel superior to such people by proclaiming the salvation of the righteous and the damnation of the rich, but just to look. Perhaps the comic picture of these rich men could even diffuse some of the hostility toward the rich reflected in Enoch's preaching. For all their pretensions and conspicuous consumption, and for all their disregard of the poor, the rich are still rather stupid bumblers who have less understanding of the Law and the prophets than the least member of the audience.

Once again, the parable appears to be framed with irenic and reconciling intent. It does not seek to fracture the community into rich against poor. It may hope to convert the rich, and also to teach the poor not to engage in the destructive envy of the rich or anger at God for not having provided them with such a fate that can all too easily increase the misery of their life. Such tensions would have to be moderated if both were to form part of a single community as they did in the early Church. And we have evidence of how difficult that combination was. Just look at the abuses that crept in at the eucharistic community meal in 1 Cor 11:17–22!

STUDY QUESTIONS

1. List three questions that a person would need to answer about the text of a parable he or she wished to interpret.

2. Look up the context for the Prodigal Son. What does the context show us about the emphasis Luke puts on the story?

3. Why is it necessary to study the historical context of a parable?

4. What does the story of the Rich Man and Lazarus tell Christians about the dangers and use of wealth? Why do you think his brothers would not have been changed "even if someone had come back from the dead"?

5. Compare the Rich Fool with the preaching in the second Enoch quotation (97:8–10). How are they similar? How is the parable different?

6. Find a contemporary situation in which concern for wealth has blinded people either to justice or to their own situation. Try to make a parable out of that situation, using one of Jesus' parables as a model.

Chapter Five

PARABLES OF GROWTH

Parables with human characters focus on their actions. The parables of growth focus on analogies derived from natural processes. Jesus uses nature metaphors to illustrate points in his preaching. The weather we share in common belongs to the exhortation to love enemies (Mt 5:45). Birds and wild flowers warn us against anxiety (Mt 6:25–33//Lk 12:22–32). These examples suggest that the parables centered on natural processes also seek to draw on our feeling for the natural world to engender trust in Jesus' vision.

Natural Processes as Foundation for Trust

Many people's lives are so divorced from the natural processes that put food on our tables or create a loaf of bread that they only relate to these parables as examples of romantic poetry. But no matter how we standardize our technology, we still cannot say exactly what the harvest will be or exactly how long it will take a particular batch of bread to rise. If you grow your own vegetables or make your own bread, you will also notice that they do not have the standardized taste from one to another which processed food does.

Nature parables seek to engage those fundamental layers of human consciousness at which we feel our relationship with nature [Wilder, 1974:141f]. One pole of that relationship represents the earth as fruitful beyond belief. It engenders the myths of natural paradise in dreams and stories the world over. The other pole is the anxiety attached to the outcome of our labor. The Old Testament used these experiences to describe that of Israel. Human activity would be fruitless without divine blessing. Jer 51:58 speaks of the futility of human labor in an oracle against Babylon. Is 55:10–11 compares the word of God to a fruitful harvest:

For as rain and snow come down from heaven
    and return not thither
but water the earth
    making it bring forth and sprout,
giving seed to the sower
    and bread to the eater,
  So shall be my word that goes forth from my mouth;
    it shall not return to me empty,
  But it shall accomplish that which I purpose,
    and prosper the thing for which I sent it.

Sower, bread, and word of God all appear again in Jesus' parables, but they do so in the smaller scale characteristic of him. He deals with the transactions between individuals and the natural world, not with the cosmic sweep of nature or her great shows of power and grandeur. God is present to the least of his creation.

Awareness of the aesthetic dimension of this appeal to nature makes it clear that these parables have more to them than might be conveyed by common interpretations such as "trust in God's future." They attach to dimensions where life and death is at stake. They awaken the relief and joy that accompanies a successful harvest. And the foundation of that relief and joy is our sense of belonging to an ordered and bountiful creation, one which is much larger than human life. Such awareness and trust may be more difficult for us who live in a time where it seems that humans may destroy the very balances that make a beneficent relationship with nature possible. Perhaps we need parables of natural process and bounty more than ever to remind us of our dependence upon the biological environment that we did not create but must respect.

The Sower (Mk 4:3–8//Mt 13:3–8//Lk 8:5–8//GTh 9)

The longest of the nature parables is also supplied with an allegorical interpretation in the synoptic gospels. GTh 9 has no such interpretation, which suggests that the parable circulated independently of the later allegory. The canonical versions show some variation. The italics in Figure 7 indicate passages that some interpreters think were added during the transmission of the parable or by Mark himself.

If the italicized passages are omitted the parable has a triadic pattern which runs through each section:

went	to sow	sowed
fell	came	devoured
fell	sprang up	withered
fell	grew	choked
fell	brought forth	yielding
thirty	sixty	one hundred

You can also see that this parable is more concerned with the seed than the Sower. His action is necessary to set up the situation for the growth of the seed.

Historical Background

When we recognize that the parable is about the seed and not the sower, debates about whether or not his method of sowing was foolish are moot. Look back at the use in Chapter One of the sower image in IV Ezra. The image is traditional. A sower sows much more seed than is actually harvested. Both Jesus and IV Ezra may have derived it from a proverb or wisdom saying about harvesting. Wisdom is often portrayed as a harvest for the wise who will wait:

> My son, from your youth up choose instruction,
>   and until you are old you will keep finding wisdom.
> Come to her like one who plows and sows,
>   and wait for her good harvest.

Fig. 7:   PARALLEL VERSIONS OF THE SOWER

MATTHEW	MARK	LUKE
	Listen!	
A sower went out to sow. And as he sowed, some seeds fell along the path,	A sower went out to sow. And as he sowed, some seed fell along the path,	A sower went out to sow his seed; and as he sowed, some fell along the path, and was trodden under foot,
and the birds came and devoured them. Other seeds fell on rocky ground where they had not much soil	and the birds came and devoured it. Other seed fell on rocky ground *where it had not much soil,* and immediately it sprang up	and the birds of the air devoured it. And some fell on the rock;
and immediately they sprang up		and as it grew up
since they had no depth of soil,	*since it had no depth of soil,*	
but when the sun rose they were scorched, and since they had no root, they withered away.	and when the sun rose it was scorched, and since it had no root, it withered away.	withered away, because it had no moisture.
Other seeds fell upon thorns, and the thorns grew up and choked them.	Other seed fell among thorns and the thorns grew up and choked it, *and it yielded no grain.*	And some fell into thorns, and the thorns grew with it, and choked it.
Other seeds fell on good soil and brought forth grain,	And other seeds fell into good soil and brought forth grain, *growing up and increasing* and yielding	And some fell into good soil and grew and yielded
some a hundred fold, some sixty, some thirty.	thirtyfold and sixtyfold, and a hundredfold.	a hundredfold.

> For in her service you will find toil a little while,
>   and soon you will eat of her produce.
> She seems very harsh to the uninstructed;
>   a weakling will not remain with her.
> She will weigh him down like a heavy testing stone,
>   and he will not be slow to cast her off.
>
> (Sir 6:18–21)

Interpreters are divided as to where the emphasis in the Sower falls. Does the final triad suggest a harvest that is enormous beyond all expectations? Or does it refer to the different yield from different ears, a normal expectation in any harvest? If the yield is normal, then the interest of the parable must lie in the types of soil. Both Is 55 and IV Ezra focus on the contrast between what is sown and what is harvested. In Isaiah the word yields a fruitful harvest just as seed does. In IV Ezra the contrast suggests that the harvest of righteous people is much smaller than what is sown. The Sower must accept loss of seed in order to insure a harvest. The final triad places the Sower on the bountiful side. Despite everything that happens to the seed, the harvest is still bountiful. Wisdom traditions like Sirach might support an interpretation that emphasizes the types of soil. It contrasts the wise who can receive wisdom's harvest because they are willing to toil and wait with the foolish, who can only find it to be an intolerable burden. The later interpretations of the parable focus on this element in the story. The comparative examples suggest that all of these dimensions of sowing might have been present to the audience when presented with such an analogy.

Teaching of Jesus

The background of the parable and its style of direct appeal to natural process both make it typical of Jesus' teaching. We see no reason to attribute it to early Christian allegorizers. The parable suggests that Jesus' vision of the presence of the rule of God can even deal with the losses that occur. The parable may have been provoked as a comment on the different responses to Jesus' preaching, or perhaps as a general comment on the claim that many are indifferent to the word of God. Look at IV Ezra again. The seer points to God's role in providing the harvest. Without favorable weather the sower can sow all the grain in the world and he still will not come up with a harvest. He asks God to deal with humans with special compassion. They are more than seeds after all. Jesus' parable might be said to counter the pessimism inherent in the common use of the image. (Sirach goes on to explain that only a few gain wisdom.) It deliberately catalogues every possible adversity and then says, "Now look how great the harvest is despite that!"

Human Significance

We often have a tendency to look for success in immediate results and statistics. Though there are some situations like planting a garden in which we don't think twice about the loss of seed (Why don't the summer squash ever hit the rock?), there are others in which the slightest failure drives us to despair. Those situations are usually ones in which we are dealing with other people. We are not so willing to be disagreed with, disliked or unpopular in such situations. We have a hard time distinguishing real success from the kind of popularity that can be measured by a poll. Sometimes that means we will not take risks that we should in addressing a situation we feel to be wrong. Yet much of Jesus' career was just that—obscurity, unpopularity, betrayal by one of his chosen twelve. The parable presents us with an image of confidence in the word of God which can take any such loss without discouragement.

Religious Significance

The parable itself opposes confidence in the word of God to human standards of immediate popularity and success. The evangelists allegorize the types of soil to present a warning to Christians lest the first enthusiasm of conversion prove fruitless. Matthew/Mark provide a fairly straightforward warning for converts. The persecutions they experience and the cares of the world are not to be allowed to dampen that faith. Matthew expands the Markan warning by making it clear that the fruit is borne in following the teaching of Jesus. He adds "understand" at the beginning and end to indicate that the people in question know what that teaching is. Many interpreters suggest that his declining sequence of numbers is also a warning against such a decline, a hint of the judgment to be faced by all.

Fig. 8:   ALLEGORICAL INTERPRETATIONS
OF THE SOWER

soil	MATTHEW	MARK	LUKE
	Hear and not understand		
		hear	
path	Evil one takes what is sown from the heart	Satan takes away	takes away
			that may not believe and be saved
rocky	receive with joy but fail due to trial and persecution on account of the word		time of temptation fall away
thorns	cares of the world and delight in riches and desire for other things		pleasures of life
	choke the word and render it unfruitful		its fruit does not mature
good	hear, understand,	hear, accept,	hold fast in honest and good heart
	and bear fruit a hundred,	bear fruit thirty, sixty,	bring forth fruit
	sixty, thirtyfold	a hundredfold	with patience

Luke's version is different. He is not concerned with the amount of harvest at all. He interprets the parable as a description of the realities of Christian life. It proceeds through the stages of that life. "Believe and be saved" refers to conversion. Specific persecution is replaced by the more general "time of temptation." Since Luke envisions Christians growing up, the thorns prevent the fruit that has begun in their conversion from ripening. Finally, the good fruit is borne by Christians who endure patiently in their faith. The whole contrasts the perils of an immature faith based on the first enthusiasm of conversion with one that has stood the various tests of Christian life. The various interpretations supplied by the evangelists not only point a lesson in the steadfastness required of the Christian, they also help the audience to see that their faith need not be shaken if they see other Christians lacking in enthusiasm. That too is part of the loss. It does not invalidate the truth of what they have received.

Seed Growing Secretly (Mk 4:26–29//GTh 21, end)

This parable tries out another implication of the sowing metaphor that was also present in the Sirach image, the patience required of the husbandman. Jas 5:7 applies that proverbial wisdom to the patience Christians must show in waiting for the coming of the Lord. The parable itself may have been developed out of proverbial wisdom about harvesting. The conclusion to GTh 21 quotes a wisdom saying that is close to the conclusion of this parable:

> Let there be among you a wise man. When the grain ripened, he came quickly with his sickle in hand and reaped it.

The wise man is like the farmer. He can take action quickly when the harvest has come.

The parable combines the motif of waiting with that of action by contrasting human activity and that of nature:

I. Human: scatter seed; go about daily business.
II. Nature: produces of itself; seed sprouts and grows.
III. Human: harvest quickly when the grain is ripe.

In the necessary, uncertain gap between sowing and harvesting all humans can do is wait. But the seeming lack of concern during that period is decisively and completely reversed at harvest time. Everyone must work as long and hard as possible. Perhaps this parable was a comment on charges like those of IV Ezra that God was not showing proper concern for the plight of his people. Or perhaps Jesus is characterizing his own ministry as that time of harvest.

Wheat and the Tares (Mt 13:24–30//GTh 57)

Matthew has this parable in place of the previous one in Mark. He interprets it as a reference to the judgment (vv. 36–43). Verses 37–39 describe the separation of the "sons of the kingdom" from the "sons of the Evil One," a dualistic expression typical of Jewish apocalyptic judgment scenes. Perhaps that interpretation came from Jewish Christian preachers. Verses 41–42 introduce a theme which is typically Matthean: Christians must remember that the Church (the field) is subject to judgment.

GTh 57 appears to abbreviate the story which would seem to be well known. Notice the summary "he did not allow them" which has replaced the initial discussion with the servants.

> The kingdom of the Father is like a man who had (good) seed. His enemy came at night and sowed weeds among the good seed. The man did not allow them to pull up the weeds. He said to them, "I am afraid that you will go to pull up the weeds and pull up the wheat along with them. On the day of the harvest, the weeds will be clearly visible, and they will be pulled up and burned."

The simpler ending of GTh may reflect the original, since Matthew's ending seems to have been expanded to fit his allegorical interpretation.

This parable is hardly a lesson in agriculture. Unlike the Seed Growing Secretly, it focuses on a series of unusual human actions: the enemy has intervened and ruined the sower's work; the servants are kept from intervening now, but referred to the harvest when they will gather the weeds to burn (probably as fuel) and harvest the wheat. The enemy's intervention makes it clear that the man was not responsible for the weeds through his own negligence.

Interpreters usually focus either on the judgment or on the patience of the husbandman, making this parable a variant of the previous one. The story emphasizes the exchange between the master and servants about the enemy's action:

    I. Two types of sowing (ND):
       man: good seed
       enemy: weeds
   II. Servant's report (DD):
       qu: didn't you sow good seed?
       ans: enemy has done it
 III. Servant's request (DD):
       qu: shall we weed the field?
       ans: no; reapers will separate

Failure to weed the field is not the only peculiar thing about the man's response. He knows that he has been the victim of an enemy's attack. In a small, village society, such a statement would also suggest that he knew or could find out who did it. Yet he neither retaliates, nor weeds the field. If GTh has preserved the original ending, the weeds are being burned as fuel. The whole story, then, may indicate that the man is cleverer than he is often given credit for: there is going to be some benefit from the enemy's attempt to harm him after all. His seed will tolerate the presence of the weeds, so rather than risk losing some of it, he will just wait. While everyone in the village is laughing at his field, he and his servants know that they will have extra fuel later.

Two religious issues seem to be involved. One is the stance of non-retaliation adopted by Jesus. (Also by God in his failure to answer prayers for a cosmic vindication against his enemies?) This man is going to turn evil into good by seeming to do nothing. The second may be shared with the previous parable—God's seeming lack of action on behalf of the righteous left in a world full of evil. The parable is quite confident that they can grow up well enough in that world and even hints that the kind of violent weeding out suggested by some people would deprive the harvest of some of the righteous who might otherwise be included.

Mustard Seed (Mk 4:30–32//Mt 13:31f//Lk 13:18f//GTh 20)

The Sower suggested that the size of the beginning sowing has nothing to do with the result. The Mustard Seed returns to issues of size. Mt 17:20 refers to the mustard seed as a proverbial example of smallness. The short version of GTh may reflect the proverbial background for the parable.

Mark's version seems to have two expansions. The double reference to sowing the seed may derive from the combination of this parable with the Sower. "Put forth branches" may also parallel the "bring forth fruit" of that parable. Without these expansions Mark/GTh have the same two-part structure, though GTh presents the parallels in a chiastic pattern: sown/smallest seed; grows up/greatest bush. The final phrase about the birds nesting in its shade emphasizes the size of the bush.

Matthew/Luke have the birds nest in the branches of a tree, not possible for a mustard bush. This change brings the proverb

Fig. 9: PARALLEL VERSIONS OF THE MUSTARD SEED

MARK

With what can we compare the kingdom of God, or what parable can we use for it?
It is like a grain of mustard seed, which when thrown on the ground is the smallest of all the seeds on the earth;
yet when it is sown,
it grows up and becomes the greatest of all shrubs, and puts forth large branches, so that the birds of the air can make nests in its shade.

GTH

It is like a mustard seed,

the smallest of all seeds.

But when it falls on tilled soil, it produces a
great plant, and

becomes a shelter for the birds of the sky.

MATTHEW

The kingdom of heaven is like

a grain of mustard which a man took and sowed in his field;
it is the smallest of all seeds,
but when it has grown,
it is the greatest of shrubs,
and becomes a tree,
so that the birds of the air come and make nests in its branches.

LUKE

What is the kingdom of God like? And to what shall I compare it? It is like
a grain of mustard seed which a man took and sowed in his garden,

and it grew,

and became a tree,
and the birds of the air
made nests in its branches.

---

into contact with an Old Testament metaphor for Israel in the messianic age—the cedar of Lebanon. Dn 4:10–12 pictures Israel as a mighty tree:

> I saw, and behold, a *tree* in the midst of the earth; and its height was *great.* The tree *grew and became* strong, and its top reached to heaven, and it was visible to the end of the whole earth. Its leaves were fair and its fruit abundant, and in it was food for all. The beasts of the field found *shade under it,* and *the birds of the air dwelt in its branches,* and all flesh was fed from it.

Later the prophecy refers to Israel's smallness among the nations as evidence that God will set the lowliest over the earth (4:17). Thus, the image of the great tree belongs to reflection about Israel's apparent insignificance, her great destiny, and God's rule over all humanity. Daniel reflects an earlier prophecy in Ez 17:22–24. God's exaltation of Israel will vindicate her against her enemies:

> Thus says the Lord God, "I myself will take a sprig from the lofty top of the cedar, and will set it out; I will break off from the topmost of its young twigs, and I myself will *plant it* upon a high and lofty mountain; on the mountain height of Israel will I plant it, that *it may bring forth boughs* and bear fruit and become a noble cedar; and under it will dwell all kinds of beasts; *in the shade of its branches birds* of every sort *will nest.* And all the trees of the field will know that I, the Lord, bring low the high tree, and make high the low tree, dry up the green tree, and make the dry tree flourish."

The imagery used in the parable has striking similarities to these prophetic reflections on the rule of God and Israel's place among the nations.

The combination of the prophetic cedar and the proverbial mustard seed is almost comic [Funk, 1975:23]. The prophetic imagery had compensated for Israel's experiences of captivity and insignificance among the nations of the world with a promise of future greatness. This greatness is being promised by the God who rules all the nations. In Jesus' time, at least two centuries after Daniel, Israel's experience was much the same as it had been under these prophets. People continued to expect exaltation and greatness to come with the manifestation of God's rule.

Jesus' parable poses a comic challenge to such images of grandeur. Cedars did not even grow in Israel. They had to be brought from Lebanon. But mustard bushes could grow up in anyone's field. Here's your national destiny, then—a mustard bush. Not as grand or glorious as the cedar, but consider what happens to all the dilemmas about the rule of God and national destiny if the nation is a mustard bush. It still can shelter the birds. The rule of God in the world is only a problem for those who think that his people have to be "top cedar." Mustard bush—that they already are. Once again Jesus has combined proverbial wisdom, allusions to great Old Testament images, and an admittedly "small scale" to recast people's images of themselves and of what it means for God to rule in the world.

This reduction also has significance for Jesus' own ministry. Willingness to stay with the small scale, the people and natural processes of the village, makes it possible to point to the presence of God's rule in a context which is quite unmessianic—messianic hopes tended to be cast as great cedars, not bushes. This parable makes it clear that Jesus is not indulging romantic appreciation for nature. He is taking on the most serious questions people had about God's rule over the world and the destiny of those who knew themselves to be his chosen people. God's rule does not have to appear in the grandiose; a mustard bush will do just as well.

Leaven (Mt 13:33//Lk 13:20f//GTh 96)

This simple comparison, which in Matthew/Luke follows the Mustard Seed, is almost identical in all the versions. It focuses simply on the contrast between the small, hidden activity of the yeast and the dramatic effect in the leavened dough which has doubled or tripled in size. Jews, who eat no yeast during the week of Passover, recognize its importance more readily than many Christians who have no idea what it is or what bread and other baked goods would be like without leavening ingredients. The amount of yeast would seem to be insignificant. The ratio in a batch of bread I made yesterday, for example, was one part yeast to a hundred and twelve parts flour, yet the loaves were somewhat more than twice their original size when they had finished rising. Rising time and other conditions also affect the taste and texture of the loaf. Yeast may not look important, but we couldn't have bread without it. Once again, the analogy reorients our imagination toward what is small. People would like to be the loaf. Perhaps they think that flour is more important, since it still appears to be part of the bread. (The yeast is the holes!) I know people who have left the yeast out of their bread, but never the flour. Yet why not be the yeast? We cannot live without it.

Summary

Jesus' nature parables are not romantic poetry. They hope to awaken us to a vision of the presence of God that is dependable even in situations that might appear to be full of loss. That does not require some grand scale to express its truth. God can take a people whose role is to be a mustard bush. His honor does not have to be defended in retaliation against enemies. Perhaps a change of perspective will even reveal useful energy in their attempted destruction. In short, the common world is pictured as a place of God's transforming presence.

STUDY QUESTIONS

1. Describe the relationship between nature parables and faith.

2. Give two examples of how the image of the Sower was used in Judaism.

3. Compare Jesus' parable of the Sower with that in IV Ezra. What do you think Jesus would say to Ezra?

4. What picture do the nature parables give us of Jesus' understanding of his own ministry?

5. Pick one of the parables from this chapter and explain what you think the significance of its message is for people today.

6. What picture do these parables give of the position and role of the righteous in the world?

Chapter Six

GOD IN PARABLES

We have seen that very simple allusions to Old Testament stories can turn proverbial wisdom or a story of somewhat comic proportions into a statement about one of the profound religious issues of the time. We have also seen that Jesus often changes the scale of such metaphors so as to point to the presence of the rule of God without demonstrations of great divine power either in human history or in natural phenomena. Thus he is able to speak of God's relationship to his people without picturing God directly.

God and the Images of Power

Many people today argue that biblical images of God as powerful king, as one who rules over slaves, and as father perpetuate various oppressive power structures by legitimating the use of power and domination in the way God acts. The Mustard Seed has already shown that the parables avoid such imagery. The Ezekiel version of the great tree pointed out that God does not support the great imperial powers but a small, oppressed people. Similarly, the biblical image of God as father appears in very specific contexts in the Old Testament. When God's people have violated the covenant and shown themselves ungrateful through their sinfulness, the prophets point out that the people is God's beloved, chosen (adopted) son. Is 63:15–19 formulates a striking image in praying for the deliverance of his people:

> Look down from heaven and see
>> from thy glorious and holy habitation.
>
> Where are thy zeal and thy might?
>> The yearning of thy heart and thy compassion
>> are withheld from me.
>
> *For thou art our Father*
>> *though Abraham does not know us*
>> *and Israel does not acknowledge us;*
>
> *Thou, O Lord, art our Father,*
>> *our Redeemer from of old is thy name.*
>
> O Lord, why dost thou make us err from thy ways
>> and harden our heart, so that we fear thee not?
>
> Return for the sake of thy servants,
>> the tribes of thy heritage.
>
> Thy holy people possessed thy sanctuary a little while;
>> our adversaries have trodden it down.
>
> *We have become like those over whom thou hast never*
>>   *ruled,*
>> *like those who are not called by thy name.*

Even Israel's physical ancestors disown a sinful Israel, God, her Father and redeemer, never will. Yet the captivity and loss felt by the people makes it seem that they have never had God as ruler or been called by his name. This image of God as father has nothing to do with patriarchy or domination. It reflects the steadfast will to save his people and a commitment even stronger than that of the ancestors of the nation [Hammerton-Kelly:20–50].

Jesus' own use of "Father" as an address to God and his instructions that the disciples do the same once again take up a prophetic image of salvation. Once again that reality is not to be experienced in the transformation of the nation's place in the world but in the experience of the individual [Hammerton-Kelly:77–81]. Though the Bible and Jesus use such metaphors for God, we should not fall into the trap of assuming that every king,

Fig. 10:   PARALLEL VERSIONS OF
THE GREAT SUPPER

MATTHEW	LUKE	GTH
The kingdom of heaven may be compared to		
a king who gave a marriage feast for his son,	A man once gave a great banquet and invited many	A man had guests
and sent his servant to call	and at the time of the banquet he sent his servants	and when he had prepared the banquet he sent his
those who were	to those who had been	servant to summon the
invited to the marriage;	invited,	guests.
but they would not come. Again he sent other servants saying, "Tell those who are invited, 'Behold, I have made ready my dinner,	"Come, for all is now ready."	He went to the first and said, "My master summons you."
my oxen and my fat calves are killed and everything is ready."		
But they made light of it, and went off: one to his farm,	But they all alike began to make excuses. The first said to him, "I have brought a field, and I must go see it.	He said, "Some merchants owe me money; they will come this evening; I will go give them orders.
	I pray you, have me excused."	I pray to be excused from the dinner."
		He went to another and said, "My master summons you."
another to his business,	And another said, "I have bought five yoke of oxen, and I go to examine them; I pray you, have me excused."	He said, "I have bought a house, and they request me for a day. I will have no time."

		He went to another and said, "My master summons you."
while the rest seized his servants, treated them shamefully, and killed them.	And another said, "I have married a wife. Therefore I cannot come."	He said, "My friend is being married, and I am to direct the banquet. I cannot come. Pray excuse me."
		He went to another and said, "My master summons you." He said, "I have bought a village and go to collect the rent. Pray excuse me."
The king was angry, and he sent his troops and destroyed those murderers and burned their city.		The servant came and said to his master, "Those whom you summoned to the banquet have excused themselves."
Then he said to his servants, "The wedding is ready, but those invited are not worthy.	Then the householder said angrily to his servant,	The master said to his servant,
Go therefore to the thoroughfares, and invite to the marriage feast as many as you find."	"Go out quickly to the streets and lanes of the city, and bring in the poor and maimed and blind and lame."	"Go to the streets; bring those whom you find so they may dine."
And those servants went out into the streets and gathered all whom they found, both bad and good,	And the servant said, "Sir, what you commanded has been done, and still there is room." And the master said, "Go to the highways and hedges and compel people to come in,	
so that the wedding hall was filled with guests.	so that my house may be filled.	
	For I tell you that none of those invited shall taste my banquet."	The buyers and the merchants shall not come into the places of my Father.

father, and master we meet in a parable is a direct image of God. It should be clear already that most of the characters are human images on a comic scale. They only image God indirectly by pointing to what happens in such human situations as similar to God's perspective. Crossan suggests that these paradoxical characters are an expression in language of a fundamental theme of biblical monotheism: God cannot be captured in images—even verbal ones [1979:117–20; 1980:58f]. We have already seen that Jesus uses some of the parables to challenge images of God that seem to have become hardened in a picture of the world which supposed that the righteous could not experience the rule of God unless there was a cosmic reversal of national destiny or dramatic judgment and punishment of sinners. God would have to defend himself since the evidence of his concern for justice rides on the fate of those people who seek to embody that justice in their lives. Jesus does not deny that God's cause in the world is closely tied to that of his faithful. But by reordering the vision of God's rule, he hopes to make it clear that God can do without such dramatic assertions of power. The presence of his rule can even take some loss [Crossan, 1980:50].

Jesus presents stories which require us to imagine God as always active, always reaching out to his people, not separated from anyone or any situation. Very common experiences may serve as a reliable guide to his rule; no detailed observance of legal prescriptions or knowledge of technical theological language is required. Even Jesus' way of speaking is non-aggressive and avoids setting up barriers between people. But this way of speaking has a powerful edge; the forgiveness and reconciliation imaged is demanded for everyone's life. The holiness appropriate to the rule of God belongs to all. It is not the property of those who have the time and education to become experts in Scripture like the Pharisees or like the Essenes, who were to spend one night in three studying it. No, this holiness is not just for the pious. It makes its claim on everyone.

The Great Supper (Mt 22:1–10//Lk 14:16–24//GTh 64)

As invitation, the parable can always be refused. Such refusal might even seem insignificant. The Great Supper suggests that a person could refuse the most important invitation of his or her life and not even recognize it. Each of the three versions has been colored by the particular message of the gospel in which it occurs. As you compare them, note the allegorical elaboration in Matthew. The supper has become a king's wedding feast for his son; the guests take much more hostile action toward the son, and the king sends out his army to retaliate—a reference to the events of the Roman destruction of Jerusalem in A.D. 70. The new people at the banquet are a mixed lot, "good and bad," who will themselves be subject to judgment. Similar allegorical elements occur in other parables of Matthew. For example, the brutal killing of some of the servants—an unlikely response to a dinner invitation—refers to the theme of the rejection of the prophets, Jesus, and probably Christian missionaries. Matthew seems to have introduced it from his allegorical expansion of the previous parable. Our survey of the characteristics of parables in different gospels [Fig. 4] indicates that Matthew likes the grand scale of kings. The simpler story of the supper in Lk/GTh is better suited to the scale of Jesus' parables. (Note that GTh has reformulated the excuses to suit the moneyed economy of his audience.)

Literary Analysis

Matthew's version has doubled the refusal of the invitation. Luke's has doubled the invitation to the surprise guests. These doublings focus our attention on different groups: Matthew on the rejected guests; Luke on those who receive a surprise invitation. Notice that in the structure of the two stories Matthew has emphasized refusal, anger and judgment:

MATTHEW		LUKE	
ND	banquet set servants sent refusal	ND	banquet set servants sent
DD	message of invitation, includes list of prepara- tions	DD	message of invitation
ND	refusal	DD	excuses given by the guests

ND	anger of the king destruction of guests	(ND)	householder speaks in anger
DD	JUDGMENT SAYING sending servants	DD	first sending of servants
ND	completed, full	DD	Completed, still room second sending, in order to fill JUDGMENT SAYING

The judgment saying serves as motivation for the sending of the servants to others in Matthew. It does not fit the allegory, since the guests have already been punished. Perhaps its relocation reflects use of the parable among Jewish Christian missionaries to legitimate their turn toward preaching to the Gentiles in the face of continued rejection by Israel. Luke, on the other hand, is more interested in the new guests. The first group represents the poor and outcast. This parable is preceded by sayings which instruct Christians to invite such people to share their banquets (Lk 14:11f).

The difference in focus reflects two directions in which the plot of the parable may be understood. Matthew takes it as a tragic warning about divine judgment. Luke's version brings to the fore the good fortune of those included by the disgruntled host. Even the final judgment saying does not preclude further relationships between the man and his friends. (Contrast Matthew's irretrievable break.) The man speaks out of a temporary but understandable anger or disappointment. You doubtless noted that Matthew makes the refusal to come an affront. The guests ignore a king's invitation, and worse yet even mistreat the servants. Luke/GTh guests offer acceptable or at least probable excuses in polite form. They do not intend to insult the host. In short, the original scale of the story presents a social disappointment or setback as an occasion of good fortune for others.

Historical Background

There are two elements in the story which can be shown to have some historical grounding—the invitation/excuses and the lesson drawn from the story that one should use such situations to do good to the poor. A Jewish story praises a tax-collector for the one good deed of his life, inviting the poor in to eat a banquet when the invited guests did not come. The double invitation in Matthew may also reflect social custom in sophisticated Jerusalem circles. One rabbinic source comments that no one in Jerusalem would attend a banquet unless invited twice (Lam Rab 4:2)—a comment on snobbery? Another saying refers to a wise guest who is dressed and ready by the second summons; the fool, on the other hand, is not ready and so excluded (Shab 153a). This saying may also be reflected in the Wedding Garment which Matthew attaches to this parable. The irony of the story is that this social elite suffered a great loss for their behavior, while a group of "no-accounts" become the guests of the king.

The excuses offered by the guests may have been intended to remind the hearer of those in Dt 20:5–7 and 24:5, a list of reasons for exempting a person from military service. If such an allusion is intended, it would strengthen the suggestion that no affront was meant by the original guests. They all have the best reasons possible not to come. Thus the focus of the story falls on the man's response to a situation in which no invited guest can come. The man turns his disappointment and anger to the benefit of others.

Teaching of Jesus

This interpretation of the story as a very human one in which the man is not God but an ordinary, disappointed host preserves the irenic tone so typical of Jesus' parables. At the same time, the parable may have served to comment on the mission Jesus was undertaking to the outcast of Israel. Rejection by some can be turned to the benefit of others. The legitimacy of excuses presented plays an important role. It means that, contrary to Matthew's view of the story as final judgment against the Jews, the door is still open to future reconciliation between the man and his friends. *This banquet* they will miss out on, but the future is not thereby closed to them.

Human Significance

We can all identify with the setting of the story. Not long ago my husband and I went to a party where half of the adults invited called with last minute excuses—illness, unexpected business trip, death in the family. Since those of us who prepared food tend to err on the generous side, we had quite a bit more than required. Some went in the freezer. The rest was taken over to people who had to stay home. No anger was involved—more amusement than anything else. Jesus' story has the man's anger and disappointment turn to the benefit of others. It suggests that even on the human level disappointment may be turned into something worthwhile if a person has the imagination to act rather than lament his or her situation.

Religious Significance

We recognize that Matthew's harsh allegory was born out of experiences of persecution and frustration with the mission to the Jews. It was easy for people to fall into the trap of seeing the destruction of Jerusalem as God's answer to their treatment of Jesus (and his disciple emissaries). Today we recognize that such a view of God and salvation history contradicts Jesus' own. He will always seek reconciliation, not condemnation. We (Gentiles) have been included in the people of God by good fortune we had no reason to expect. What remains for God's original people is still an open possibility, as the original parable suggests.

Luke's application of the parable points to important social concerns. Christians must use their abundance to aid the poor and outcast with the same determination shown by this man. He will not rest until every place is filled. There is no room to sit back and assume that enough has been done.

Wedding Garment (Mt 22:11–14)

This additional parable may have been derived from the saying about the wise and foolish guest being dressed when the call comes or caught short. Here a man has come to the feast without proper attire. Matthew has combined it with the Wedding Feast to warn the "bad and good" inside that they will be judged. Verses 13f are typical Matthean judgment language. Perhaps the original parable was a proverbial assertion of the certainty of judgment prefaced by "What do you think?" If a host will not let a guest get by with such an affront, will God fail in his judgment?

Places at Table (Lk 14:7–11)

These sayings form a double with the Great Supper. Prov 25:6f gives potential courtiers the following advice:

> Do not put yourself forward in the king's presence or stand in the place of the great; for it is better to be told, "Come up here," than to be put lower in the presence of the prince.

Social calculations based upon one's place of honor or lack of it were a common part of social behavior in ancient society. One might show disdain for a person by seating him or her in a low place. Though such behavior among the rich and those who sought to advance socially was often held up to scorn, it was a pervasive feature of life. Luke has to reconcile wealthier members of the community to concern for, even willingness to invite, the poor and those with whom they would normally not associate. Perhaps the original use of such sayings was associated with Jesus' own concern that his disciples not adopt such trappings of rank and privilege as were typical of the "great people" (e.g. Mk 10:42–44).

Summary

This group of parables plays on awkward situations of social etiquette with benign humor. They challenge us to ask what really counts in such situations. Perhaps some of the norms that we adopt from our society should not be so quickly taken up. Holding ourselves to such standards may bar us from responding to the more pressing standards of justice, concern for the poor and outcast, or possibly even fellowhsip with all members of the Christian community. Our social habits of boundaries, status, insult and hierarchy are no concern of God's.

STUDY QUESTIONS

1. What does the Old Testament mean when it refers to God as Father?

2. How do we learn about God in the parables?

3. What does Matthew's allegorical interpretation of the Great Supper say about the fate of the Jews as people of God? Why would he have reached that conclusion? Why have Christians today come to reject it?

4. Why are lessons about "social behavior" challenged by Luke's presentation of the Great Supper and Places at Table?

5. Find a modern example of the social dilemma presented in one of the three parables. Try turning it into a parable, using Jesus' example as a model.

6. What conclusions would you expect a person to draw from your parable? Why?

Chapter Seven

ALLEGORY: WHEN IS A PARABLE NOT A PARABLE?

The Great Supper provided an excellent example of how the open-ended character of the parable as story lent itself to adoption by different Christian communities to meet new experiences and crises. Matthew's version of the story was particularly laden with allegory. Usually the evangelists limit their interpretations to small additions—sayings at the end of a parable, and the context in which the parable is set. In cases such as the Sower and the Wheat and Tares, the evangelists give us examples of allegorical interpretations of the parables that are quite independent of the stories themselves. The most common allegory is to apply God/word of God/Jesus to the central character or central item in a parable and Christians or various classes of humans to those who react or fail to react to the situation provided by the story. Various interpretations of the same parable show us that early Christians used the allegory as an important way to bring out the meaning of stories for themselves. Some allegorical elements may be introduced into a story by allusions to great Old Testament images: shepherd/sheep for God and his people, the cedar of Lebanon, or even a banquet for salvation with God such as we find in Is 25:6. One does not need to be conscious of these images to appreciate some of the dynamics of the stories. Some interpreters deny their presence altogether. But they do make the parables part of the ongoing discussion about God and salvation. They remind us that these stories are part of a larger discussion of God's relationship to his people. They are not simply prudential wisdom or humorous observations about human behavior.

Parable and Allegory

These examples have already shown you that the parables are not the kind of allegory which one cannot understand without a complex system to decode the characters. Allegorical interpretation of Homer, the Bible and even ancient myths was widely practiced among the educated of Jesus' time. They used allegory to show that stories which did not appear to have much significance were really teaching deep truths of philosophy. Abraham represents the soul on its journey toward God, for example. The Essenes interpreted Old Testament prophecies as references to the history of their own sect in allegorical form. Unless a person were a member of the sect the person could not really understand what the prophets were referring to. The early Christians made a similar interpretation of prophetic texts—and some parables—in terms of the life of Jesus and the later history of their community. Since the parables themselves do not require such allegorization, many interpreters assume that every time one finds allegorical features in the parables, they represent the interpretative activity of early Christian preachers.

However, it does not seem fair to reduce all such allegorical allusions to later preaching. The images that are traditional with the audience would make some allegory a natural. Thus interpreters have come to distinguish between use of allegory in a parable and treating the whole story as an allegory. Allegory plays an important role in religious literature. Crossan [1976:115–126; 1980:96–102] has pointed out that several of these functions are quite different from the role played by allegorical allusion in the parables of Jesus:

(1) There is no evidence that allegory is being used to disguise the teaching of a sect in order to escape persecution by re-

ligious or political authorities, as may have been the case in Daniel, for example.

(2) There is no indication that Jesus wants his teaching to be a secret from outsiders, something that can only be understood by those who have the code to use in allegorical interpretation.

(3) There is no indication that the parable is considered an inferior form of teaching, one which the educated can understand as "philosophy for the masses" or the like.

(4) There is no indication that the universe is presented as a tissue of allegorical relationships which are mirrored in human nature. One finds some medieval authors arguing that since the creator made such a "multi-level" universe, his divinely inspired book, the Bible, must also have levels of teaching from the historical to the ethical to the eschatological to the mystical. Allegorical interpretation proves the divinity of Scripture. All of these functions of allegory play an important role in the interpretation of religious traditions, but they are hardly suited either to the context of Jesus' ministry or to the allegorical interpretations that we do find among early Christians.

Crossan suggests that we need a different category to apply to Jesus' use of allegory. He calls it "ludic" allegory. The parable plays with its plot. It examines the various possible outcomes of human situations and cuts across different levels of human and social reality. Allegory can be viewed as part of the multiple interpretations that can be explored in any given parable. When earlier interpreters rejected allegorization of the parables, they were really rejecting the idea that a parable has a single message that can be neatly capsulized in a moral lesson. Such moral lessons too easily become expressions of the personal theology of the preacher or theologian. The most common examples one meets today are those which treat all the central figures as direct images of God rather than as direct images of humans and only an indirect pointing to God. [See, for example, Schillebeeckx, 1979:161–69, and the critique of the assumption that all parables are statements about the Rule of God in Breech:16–29.] What is necessary is to preserve the dynamic character of the parables and their direct way of using ordinary human life and wisdom to point out the larger realities involved in those lives. Allegorical allusions may even be a key feature of that suggesting pointing. Crossan points out that such creative use of allegory is quite different either from the moral interpretations of the rabbinic tradition or from the allegorical interpretations which we know come from the early Church. When faced with allegorical elements in a parable, one should see if they can be fitted into this pattern of creative story-telling. If they can, then the presumption should be on the side of authenticity.

Ten Virgins (Mt 25:1–13); Shut Door (Lk 13:24–30); Faithful Servants (Lk 12:35f)

The Ten Virgins is a prime case for those who seek an example of a parable that is created by early Christian allegorical preaching. It belongs to a series of parables on the judgment by which Matthew warns his readers that they must be prepared no matter how long it is before the day of judgment comes. Masters, who are slow to come, always turn up unexpectedly (20:30f; 20:36f, 50f; 25:19–21, 31–33). These parables warn that judgment will divide faithful from unfaithful Christians (24:40f; 25:14–30; 25:31–46). The concluding verse of this parable (v. 13) is a typical Matthean warning. But notice that it contrasts with the parable itself. The wise virgins are not condemned for sleeping. The cry "Lord, open to us!" and the expression used against those who say "Lord, Lord" also seems typically Matthean (cf. 7:21—those who make such a cry are not saved in the judgment unless their works show the fruits required of a disciple).

Those who think that the whole parable was created by early Christian preachers point to other difficulties within the story itself. The introduction (v. 1) has the virgins going to meet the bridegroom while v. 6 has him suddenly arriving on the scene. They point out that "then" is used to refer to the second coming in 24:44. They argue that the only way to make sense of this parable is to see it as an allegory for Matthew's theology of the judgment. The good servant in Mt 24:45 parallels the prudent virgin 25:2, 4. The story turns on oil or lack of it. That detail seems to require allegorization. It must represent the good deeds, the fruit required in Mt 7:16–20 [Donfried, 1974]. Such an allegorical rendering is said to solve other difficulties in the narrative. The wise virgins seem to be poor examples of charity, since they refuse to share their oil. If the oil refers to good works, then there is no possibility that they could have shared it. The suggestion that they go to the dealers cannot have had any realistic application in the time of Jesus and must only belong to the allegorical level of the story, which says that it is impossible to come up with the required works. Thus the whole reflects the kind of theology of judgment expressed in Mt 7:21–23. The conclusion may also have been taken from the parable of the Shut Door (Lk 13:25–27).

Without denying that Matthew has interpreted this parable as a warning to Christians about the judgment and is responsible for much of its language, we should see if the same materials might not lead to another reading of the story. One difficulty faced by interpreters of this parable is that we lack reliable information about wedding customs [Jeremias:171ff]. Thus, it is not possible to sort out the puzzling features of the story on the basis of a cultural example. We have to try to make sense of the story as we have it. The conclusion, vv. 11b–12, is very close to the conclusion of the Shut Door in Lk 13:25-27. It may represent a combination of that parable with one which simply ended with the shutting of the door in v. 10. The audience would know as soon as the door of the house was shut that the foolish virgins would not be able to get into the feast—at least not without drawing a great deal of attention to themselves! Like the guests who refused the invitation to the Great Supper, they have excluded themselves [see Smith:116f].

Other items in this parable parallel the story of the Good Servant which comes immediately before it in Matthew. The key figure is delayed; no one knows when he will arive; there is a right and wrong response to the situation of delay, and the good servant like the wise virgin exemplifies the proper vigilance that should characterize the time of waiting [so Meier:175]. Such parallels are not surprising if one recognizes that the whole section has been extensively rewritten by Matthew to form a complete discourse on the judgment. If we look at the parallel material in Lk 12:35f we find that we have one of those simpler illustrations of part of the dynamics of the parable that we find so frequently in the parables collection. The image is one of servants waiting with burning lamps for their master's return from a marriage feast. Since it is late, the master will have to come and knock to find his servants ready inside. Luke's context also expands the parable with other sayings about delay; perhaps the master will not even return until dawn (vv. 37-39). This simpler parable has the feature of burning lamps (oil) which other interpreters have insisted only make sense when they are allegorized. However, the whole implication of the virgins' story is that any prudent person would have had the required oil. The wise virgins brought enough with them to last the whole night. They were not carrying extra as insurance. But all the servant sayings and stories also reflect the common knowledge that there are lazy servants who are not prepared.

If we take this story as a hint along with the fact that in v. 6 the bridegroom appears to be arriving at his own residence after the delay, the contours of the parable begin to become clear. The Lukan story suggests that in the opposite situation masters might find themselves banging on their own doors to awaken slumbering and unprepared servants. The ten virgins of this story should be seen as servants, not as guests. In that case, the story represents a somewhat more extended example of the type. The wedding motif here has been shifted. Instead of the master returning late from someone else's feast, he seems to be returning with the bride (and his friends) for his own feast. (Cp. Jn 2:1-11 where the feast is at the bridgegroom's home.)

Literary Analysis

The simpler analogy in Luke enables us to see the structure of this story behind the allegorical elaborations that it has received from its context. The delay is a necessary feature of the plot. Unlike the Lukan analogy which focuses on the "good servant," this story focuses on the plight of the foolish one:

ND (vv. 1-5) Set the scene: waiting; contrast wise/foolish.
DD (v. 6f) Cry wakes up the household.
DD (v. 8f) Foolish try to get oil from the wise.
ND (v. 10) Foolish are excluded.

The repetition of the expression lamp/oil is used to focus attention on the foolish. They are introduced first and the addition of material about the shut door (vv. 11f) emphasizes their exclusion. Repetition of expressions about coming in/going out focuses the dynamics of the story on inside/outside the house. Verses 1–6 are framed with *come out to meet*. The foolish *go out to buy* (vv. 9f) while all the rest *go in* (v. 10). This dynamism lends finality to the shutting of the door.

Perhaps the story should really be called that of the foolish virgins since the rhetoric of the story focuses our attention on them. They are scurrying off to try to find oil not because they are negligent guests, nor even because the feast could not go on without their five lamps, but because they have been trapped as negligent servants who are clearly likely to suffer their master's wrath. One can picture them scrambling off down the street, perhaps even pushing their way through the party arriving for the wedding banquet. Once one recognizes that this parable is about a group of ill-prepared servants, there is no need to allegorize the oil. Nor is there any reason for the objection that the wise virgins should have shared. If they had done that and all of them had been unprepared, they all would have been in trouble. Anyone in the audience can recognize the type of servants involved and the crisis which is confronting them. They are trying at the last minute to get out of a situation that they knew they should have been prepared for. Once the door is shut it is clear that they will not pull off their attempts to get out of a scolding or worse, though one can also imagine them thinking that perhaps they will still manage to rouse a fellow servant inside and sneak back in before their absence is noticed. The conclusion from the Shut Door in vv. 11f might reflect that situation—in which case they have made two vain attempts to bail themselves out. First, they tried to talk their fellow servants into helping them. Second, they went off to buy some new oil (and apparently succeeded in doing so) and tried to get back in after the door had been shut. But they are faced with bad luck there too. The master himself comes to open the door. Thus, though the plot is something of a tragic one, this story has the same sort of comic edge that we observed in the story of the Rich Man and Lazarus. The foolish servants do not have any idea of what their real situation is. They persist in showing their foolishness by their attempts to bail themselves out at the last minute. Those attempts fail because it really is the last minute. So understood, this parable fits in with the scale and imaginative creativity so typical of Jesus' parable telling.

Teaching of Jesus

This parable clearly belongs to a series of parables and observations about good and bad servants. It also has affinities with the Great Supper and the Rich Man and Lazarus because in both instances the characters who find themselves excluded at the end of the parable are excluded due to their own decisions and actions. They clearly had the opportunity to respond appropriately to the invitation or to the need of the poor person or to the necessity to be prepared. Both the foolish virgins and the rich man are a bit pathetic in their attempts to salvage the situation once it has been lost. The audience is familiar enough with both scenarios to recognize the absurdity of their behavior. Perhaps Jesus told this parable to illustrate his own mission. Perhaps he wanted to indicate that people will always fall into two camps, wise and foolish—a division frequently used in the wisdom literature. One should not be surprised that some people are not concerned about what God expects of humanity. The foolish always act like this. They are always unprepared, and they always expect to bail out at the last minute.

Human Significance

The story is clearly about types of people we all know. Anyone can give examples of people who do not make the kind of preparations that are required and then go around trying to scrounge from friends to get out of the jam that they have landed themselves in. Students do it at school, people do it in the various social relationships that they have—there is always someone in a crowd known to be unreliable when it comes to doing his or her part for a group outing—and people do it at work. Those of us who are frequently beset by such a person could not help cheering the outcome of this story. We all find ourselves hoping that the boom gets lowered somewhere along the line on people like that even if we do help the person out of whatever jam he or she is in. We also all know that such people seem to be oblivious to the effect that their behavior has on others. They can usually be counted on to do the same thing again, and again. That makes such a person different from the friend who is in an occasional jam and needs some assistance to get out of it. We know that that person's crisis is legitimate and that that person will bail us out when we find ourselves in a rough spot. The foolish, on the other hand, can never be trusted even for that. They simply are not ready. This parable shows such people at their worst, though it also gives an answer on the part of the wise that many of us should probably use on occasion but don't. They point out that they cannot part with any of their oil, and suggest an alternate course of action. The story assumes that their suggestion was a possibility, since they did obtain the oil. That solution, however, forces the responsibility for being unprepared back onto the foolish virgins. In the final analysis, they are caught in their stupidity. They might have done better to wait outside until morning rather than call attention to themselves by their banging on the door.

Religious Significance

The elements of judgment which Matthew's allegory adds to the story are not entirely absent from the dynamics of the parable. After all it does show us some foolish people being caught in the consequences of their actions. If people can be so foolish in their everyday lives, then it is no wonder that people can act in the same way when it comes to religious issues. After all, those do not confront us with the consequences of neglect as rapidly as these foolish servants find themselves shut out. Perhaps somewhere even in our lifetime the kind of character that we develop if we neglect the virtues and concerns that are the issues in religious teaching gets us into situations where we are unhappy and we recognize that maybe we should have paid attention to such questions earlier. But it often might seem that there is no penalty for neglect in that sphere. Even those who are prudent in making the required preparations in the rest of their lives can be afflicted by such questions. Peter voices the question in Mk 10:28, "What about us?" He is assured that discipleship will have its rewards.

Summary

This parable turns out to be a good example of how Jesus could speak about responsibility and judgment in such a way as to not exclude those whom he might be warning. Its tone is quite different from that of Matthew's allegory, since it chooses to show up the unprepared as comic and rather foolish, rather than condemn them to eternal doom. Public embarrassment and a scolding from the master are the punishments pictured here. The story also suggests that the difference between wise and foolish is not some unusual effort suddenly made by the wise but the result of habitual types of behavior. The foolish always behave like this. Now they are in a situation where that type of habitual behavior lands them in the soup. It is very easy to convert such a story into the kind of vengeful judgment preaching that we expect of religious people. We all know people who would not respond as the wise did but would deliver a long oration on their foolish behavior as soon as the virgins asked for oil. One of the things that turns many people away from religion is this attitude of self-righteous preaching on the part of the good people.

Jesus' ability to speak about responsibility for our actions and even about judgment in a comic rather than a condemnatory tone must have been an important part of his appeal to sinners and to those who felt that their standards of religious practice would not measure up to the stricter preaching of the Pharisees. The ability to take such a position is also crucial to other facets of Jesus' preaching such as his warnings against judging others and his insistence on love of enemy. A non-judgmental or non-retaliatory posture allows enemies a chance to open communication with you. It allows the sinners the possibility of approaching Jesus. The benign humor with which Jesus portrays the fate of the foolish also has something to say to the righteous. They should not get caught in the trap of hostility or resentment toward the foolish or sinners. The latter will come to their due reward/fall soon enough. The disciple does not need to waste time and energy worrying about how God is going to manage things. We might even try to apply the lesson on the human level. We all know good, responsible employees who seem to waste vast amounts of emotional energy lamenting the behavior of others who are not performing their job as they should. The parable does not suggest that we should always bail such people out. It suggests that maybe we should suggest ways to them of shouldering their own responsibility. Beyond that there are better things to do with one's time and emotional energy than fretting about someone else who is not doing his or her job. Habitual action of that sort will eventually come to its crisis. We really do not have to worry about it. Nor should we let such behavior deter us from our own path. Matthew may have had to intensify his judgment language to warn Christians who were being tempted to take such a position of casual concern with their religion.

STUDY QUESTIONS

1. Give two examples of how early Christians use allegory to interpret the parables.

2. What makes a parable different from an allegory?

3. How does "ludic allegory" differ from the use of allegory in interpretations such as that given the Sower?

4. Write your own dialogue between the wise and foolish virgins. Can you think of any other outcomes for the initial situation?

5. Find a modern example for the situation imaged in the Ten Virgins. What general conclusions about human beings does that situation suggest?

6. Why does Jesus give a comic edge to his images of judgment? Why has Matthew sharpened the judgment language of the parables?

Chapter Eight

THE GOOD SAMARITAN:
PARABLE OF THE LOVE COMMAND

Christians are so used to summarizing the teaching of Jesus as "love your enemies" (Mt 5:38–48/Lk 6:27–36) that they are often surprised to learn that other religions have similar teaching. The wisdom tradition of the Old Testament suggested that one should treat an enemy with kindness:

> If your enemy is hungry, give him bread to eat;
>   and if he is thirsty give him water to drink;
> For you will heap coals of fire on his head,
>   and the Lord will reward you.
>
> (Prov 25:21f)

Jesus' teaching about love of enemies occurs in a section that warns disciples against the dangers of anger, and judgment. The wisdom tradition also had teaching about such problems:

> Anger and wrath, these also are abominations,
>   and the sinful man will possess them.

He that takes vengeance will suffer vengeance from
the Lord,
and he will firmly establish his sins.
Forgive your neighbor the wrong he has done,
and then your sins will be pardoned when you pray.
Does a man harbor anger against another,
and yet seek for healing from the Lord?
Does he have no mercy toward a man like himself,
and yet pray for his own sins?
If he himself being flesh maintains wrath,
who will make expiation for his sins?
Remember the end of your life, and cease from enmity;
remember destruction and death and be true to the
commandments.
Remember the commandments and do not be angry
with your neighbor;
remember the covenant of the Most High and overlook ignorance.

(Sir 27:30–28:7)

The summary of the Law as love of God and neighbor, which also
appears in the teaching of Jesus (e.g. Lk 10:25–28 where it serves
to introduce the parable of the Good Samaritan) is also known
from Jewish writings of the time of Jesus:

Love the Lord through all you life, and one another with
a true heart. (T Dn 5:3)

Love the Lord and your neighbor. Have compassion on
the poor and the weak. (T Iss 5:2)

These examples from Jewish wisdom traditions [see Fuller,
1978:52] show that Jesus is not telling his audiences something
that they have not heard before. The wisdom traditions recognized the commandment of love as a summary of the Law. They
also recognized the destructive effects of anger and suggested
that to forgive others was a condition for receiving forgiveness
from God. It would be more appropriate to say that Jesus focuses
on these traditions as the epitome of God's will for humanity
than to claim that only Christians have teaching of this sort.

You can see that two types of love command are part of the tradition. Both appear in the teaching of Jesus. The first concerns love between members of the same community—neighbors. In the New Testament such formulations of the love command refer to the love which Christians should show to one another. This love is not a matter of sentiment but of concrete action: hospitality, assistance to the poor, care for the helpless of the community—all the things that the Old Testament had insisted were fundamental to Israel as a covenant people. Read Rom 12:9–20, 15:7, and Jas 2:14–17 for examples of how love was preached and practiced among early Christian communities.

Love of Enemies and Social Context

The second formulation of love of enemies derives from the larger social context of reflection on anger and vengeance. Roman historian Peter Brown has noted the destructive effects of feuds in society of the time. People lived in close-knit, face-to-face communities which were constantly threatened by outbreaks of anger and hostility [Brown:40f, 83–90]. The examples from the wisdom tradition show such concerns. People often think that the saying from Proverbs is only a way of saying that if you don't take vengeance yourself, God will do a much better job than you ever could. They rightly reject such an attitude. But consider that same advice from the perspective of a social order that is constantly threatened by outbreaks of anger and by the long-term feuds that could result. You can see that its aim is to moderate such violence. Most of us have little experience of the kind of anger, hostility and enmity that can result when people live in the close quarters of a village or a crowded city quarter where one's family has lived for generations. We can be insulted by someone and it will pass in our society unnoticed. That is hardly possible in the world from which these traditions come. Retaliation is often required as a defense of one's own and one's family's honor. Thus, it is no simple matter for a person to be told "Don't seek vengeance" when he or she has been wronged or insulted. You can also see that, like love of neighbor, love of enemy addresses concrete social situations. It has nothing to do with some sentiment about the enemy. It asks people to behave in a way different from usual, and yet one which may prove of great benefit for the whole social group.

Problems of enmity are even more intense in Palestine. Several hostile groups live side by side. It is one thing perhaps to apply such teaching to the enemy who is a member of one's own village or neighborhood; it is quite another to extend it to the real enemies that surround one. The native population consisted of three groups. There were the Gentiles who had settled in various cities in the area. Such people might be a mixture of the indigenous populations of the area who had never been completely driven out by Jewish conquest and the Greeks who settled there after the conquest of Alexander the Great in the fourth century B.C. There were Samaritans who represented people left in the north of Israel after the Assyrian conquest in the eighth century B.C. They had their own version of the Law of Moses and their own places of worship, and they refused to acknowledge the Judaism centered in the Jerusalem temple. Perhaps because they were also claiming to be descendants of Abraham and true followers of the Law of Moses and because they lived in closer proximity—though in separate villages—to the Jews, violence between those two groups was frequent. "Samaritan" seems to have been a term of insult when applied by one Jew to another. If you read Lk 9:51 or Jn 4:9 you can see examples of the relationships between the two groups. All three groups were under the rule of the real outsiders, the Romans. Sporadic violence and repression were constant realities of life under Roman rule. Lk 13:1f refers to a typical example of such violence. Pilate's willingness to crucify Jesus is another example. Palestinians living in occupied territory in Israel today have much the same feeling when they see an Israeli soldier that a Jew of the time of Jesus would have had on seeing a Roman one—or a fellow Jew who was working for the Romans in some capacity. You need only pick up the newspaper to get a feel for the level of violence in the region. People who live there recognize that the violence with which they live today is part of thousands of years of warfare and suffering in a land where one seems constantly surrounded by enemies.

In such a context, love of enemies is not the kind of passive, "sissy" behavior that some people feel it to be. If it is meant to apply beyond the confines of an enemy who belongs to one's own village, social or racial group, then it is aimed at one of the most critical problems of human society; certainly one of the most critical in the Middle East. Ancient philosophers sometimes preached love of enemies as well. They understood it as practical advice for three classes of people [see Schottroff, 1978]:

(1) The slave or conquered person might as well "love," cooperate with his enemy and suffer the injustice of the master. This attitude is preferable to the punishments that would otherwise result. Look at 1 Pt 2:18ff or Col 3:25. Such advice was applied to Christian slaves. But you will see that the Christians had a slightly different motivation. They hoped that such behavior would help convert the masters. Their religion was persecuted enough; they could not afford to give people cause for taking any more action against them.

(2) Rulers were advised to show clemency to a conquered enemy. The king might actually increase his hold over the conquered territory if the conquered realized that he had spared them a fate that they otherwise would have expected as conquered.

(3) Cynic philosophers who wandered about criticizing the ills of society invoked his image for martyrdom from refusal to accept injustice or to refrain from speaking against the corruption of rulers and society. They would refrain from showing hostility toward those who persecuted them for their preaching as an example of philosophic detachment from all that society might try to do to a person. One might say that love of such enemies was an example of the strength of their philosophy.

These analyses of love of enemy represent specific advice for certain classes of people: slaves; kings; philosophers. The New Testament only mentions one such view, the advice to slaves. That may have been taken from such common reflection, though you will also notice that it has been given a new Christian focus. The slave has an example in Christ himself. He also has an important reason for his obedience, since it contributes to the overall spread of the gospel.

The example of the interpretation of advice to slaves suggests another possibility: Christians generally may have interpreted love of enemies as an active, missionary position. It certainly had application to their situation, since there are many examples in the New Testament of persecution faced by those who preached the gospel. But Jesus' commandments are not just limited to that level of Christian activity. They refer to all the levels of violence in the society in which people found themselves. Jesus consistently refuses to sponsor participation in the dynamics of violence in any form. We have already seen that his stories are carefully told so as not to provoke the imagination of violence that can easily take hold of a conquered or oppressed people.

The Good Samaritan (Lk 10:29–37)

The title given this parable points to the striking character of its plot. Imagine after the almost daily occurrences of Jewish/Arab violence that someone were to tell a story of the Good Palestinian to a Jewish audience. Such a story would certainly provoke a number of conflicting reactions. After all the story does not even permit the Jew to be the one who shows the extraordinary kindness. Most of us are more willing to imagine ourselves showing some extraordinary benefit to an enemy than we are to imagine that the enemy would ever do the same for us.

We only have one version of this parable. It is set in the context of the debate over the commandment of love of neighbor— a story which occurs in the other gospels without this parable (see Mt 22:34–40; Mk 12:28–31). This particular section of Luke is the beginning of Jesus' journey to Jerusalem. The section was initiated with a reference to hostility between Samaritans and Jews (9:51). It is linked together with verbs of coming and going (9:51, 57; 10:1, 3, 38). The action of the parable suits that context, since the man is going down from Jerusalem to Jericho, a direction opposite to that of Jesus and his disciples who are on their way up to Jerusalem [see Crespy: 28; this section is set off from its context by the high incidence of such verbs of motion]. One might almost imagine Jesus and his disciples passing along by the man in question.

However, the insertion of the parable at this point in the story creates certain anomalies. The lawyer sets out to ask a legal question: What is the extent of the term "neighbor" in the love command? You can see from our earlier reflections on the problems of enmity in society that such a question is not a trivial one. It may have been even more of an issue for Luke's audience, since the Christian community itself brought together people of such widely differing backgrounds that none of the usual social norms of defining the neighbor and my obligations to him or her would apply. Luke may have seen this parable as an important one for instructing Christians on their obligations to view all members of the community as neighbor. The application of the parable to the legal question of what the commandment means by neighbor may even have been part of the form in which Luke found it in the tradition [so Crossan, 1973a:60f]. Such applications of parables to points of interpretation in the Law are, as we have seen, typical of parables in the rabbinic tradition. Lk 10:37 makes it clear that this parable is now considered an example for Christians to imitate. A Gentile audience would, of course, identify more readily with the Samaritan than Jesus' Jewish audience would have done. If they failed to identify with the Jew in the ditch, then they might have missed the emotional turmoil that the parable could cause a Jewish audience altogether.

Literary Analysis

Lk 10:36 might also have been part of the legal application of the parable. The original might not have been concerned with love of neighbor at all but with the teaching on enemies. Aside from the difficulty that many modern people have in identifying with the Jew in the ditch, modern interpreters often inject contemporary anti-clericalism back into this story. They assume that the audience would have sneered "How typical!" as the priest and Levite passed by [Funk, 1974b:78]. We should question such modernizing. The more common complaints were that the clergy were "defiled" by their lack of adherence to the purity stipulations of the Law—one of which required that priests avoid contact with a corpse, which this man certainly seemed to be. The Levite would only have to do so if he were on his way up to Jerusalem to do his tour of service in the temple. If he were on his way back home, he could have helped the man [Jeremias:203f, who gives an anti-clerical reading]. An audience without anti-clerical prejudices might have assumed that both were on their way to the temple. An anti-clerical interpretation only makes sense if we assume that Jesus told the story in a context critical of ritual duties which blind people to higher obligations of love—as seems to be the situation in some of the controversies over healing on the Sabbath.

Since this story does not demand such an anti-clerical interpretation, we can simply take vv. 29b–32 as introductory. The fact that the first two passers-by cannot help because they cannot see if the man is dead or not only heightens the tension. What is going to happen to the man? The audience might presume that he will not die in a ditch. Otherwise, why start the story? If the introduction has heightened the apprehension of the audience, imagine their reaction when a Samaritan is next over the horizon. The best they might hope for is that the Samaritan will not see him—but the priest and the Levite did so. It looks as though the man's life is in dire jeopardy. Perhaps the Samaritan will look to see if he is alive, and, if so, kill him. Perhaps, he will just pass by like the others, and the man will die after all, an unlucky victim of the travelers who happened to be on the road that day.

Most of the parable is devoted to describing the surprising action taken by the Samaritan. He goes far beyond the minimal steps required to save the man's life. He personally sees to it that the man receives everything needed to return to health. Thus, his compassion not only overcomes the enmity between himself and the Jew, but even the normal reluctance to spend one's resources aiding a stranger. One could even say that he treats the man as though he were one of his own relatives. The Samaritan's section of the story could be represented by the following actant diagram:

Compassion turns out to be much stronger than the emnity that is fostered by the social relationships between the two groups. The earlier encounter with the priest and Levite might be described as:

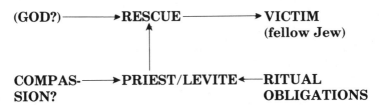

Though the story is not explicitly hostile to the interpretation of the Law that keeps the priest and Levite from helping the man, the Samaritan's action does create some ambiguity. Is it possible that the enemy can be more a "fellow" than those from one's own group?

Other interpreters trace the ambiguities inherent in this story to the confusion that a Jewish audience might feel. They would begin, of course, by identifying with the man in the ditch. The story is designed to provoke anxiety over whether or not the man will be rescued. But the long-standing hostility between the two groups might still make it difficult to imagine being aided by a Samaritan. The reversal in this story's plot really takes place because of that identification with the victim. His good fortune turns out to be derived from the fact that compassion has led his enemy to act as a friend/almost a relative. The man so helped may have been as embarrassed as he was grateful. The story leaves us with that question. What did the victim do when he got well enough to realize what had happened? Did he leave and go on his way to Jericho? Did he wait until the Samaritan returned in order to thank him? What did he tell his friends? Did the incident have any effect on his views of Samaritans later?

Teaching of Jesus

The parable represents a striking side of Jesus' teaching about love of enemies. The possibility of doing so ultimately resides in a refusal to see the enemy as such. The incident over the Samaritan village in 9:51 captures the spirit behind this story. The disciples want Jesus to use his miraculous powers to teach a thing or two to the Samaritans who refuse hospitality to their group. Jesus refuses and passes on. Such a refusal might well be expected, given the non-judgmental tone of many of his stories. This parable unveils a deeper side to that attitude. It is willing to cast the "enemy" so-called as a morally superior person. The Samaritan in the story emerges as a person whose compassion could not be exceeded by anyone. Part of Jesus' ability to perceive reality in this way belongs to another feature of his stories. This story is not about Jews and Samaritans as classes but about a single, helpless Jewish victim and a single, well-off Samaritan—probably a merchant of some kind who regularly traveled that road on business. As individuals a Samaritan might befriend a Jew in this way. The parable seeks to suggest love of enemy to the audience by asking them to identify not with a Jew who showed such extraordinary generosity and compassion to an enemy but with the victim in the ditch. Perhaps, finally, that is the only way that the required change of heart can be experienced. A person cannot really abolish the category of "enemy" as long as he or she looks on the enemy from a position of superiority that justifies the relationship between the two groups on the grounds that "our group" is morally superior to yours and hence justified in our hatred of you. One can only make the required change of heart if one really acknowledges the equality or here even the superiority of the enemy. Then one may acknowledge that the enemy too can be an equal. Of course, in this context the enemy is no longer really an enemy. The Samaritan's compassion has completely erased all such concerns from his behavior. The Jew in the ditch is no longer an enemy but simply a helpless victim for whom the Samaritan has compassion and the resources to help.

Human Significance

One can hardly avoid being struck by this story's depth when one looks at the lines of enmity that cross the various regions in the Middle East today, most bolstered by the language and claims of religion on the various sides of the conflict. Of course, the story can paint its striking lesson precisely because it does not try to reform the situation by addressing the Jewish/Samaritan problem but by picturing the audience's enemy in a surprising act of compassion. Yet the story also suggests that the problem falls in the failure to find a category outside that of enmity which divides the warring sides. Enemies who are still enemies after some peace settlement will still view each other with the hostility and destruction that can break out in violence at any time. They must be able to find a common ground of concern and compassion that does not trade on the old images of enmity.

Closer to home, we can also see that the parable does not view people in categories. In practical terms, that also suggests that anyone who is truly compassionate will not respond to others in terms of social or racial classes. Nor is it possible to excuse failure to act with compassion on the grounds that the victim is an enemy, or not of a particular sex, racial or ethnic group.

Many of our solutions to such problems of injustice and inequality are unable to avoid intensifying the symbols and boundaries that divide groups of people. But those very divisions can have a backlash in that they may make it more difficult for individuals to cross the boundaries and recognize people of the other groups as "non-enemies," as objects of the same compassion and generosity that we might show to members of our own families.

Religious Significance

This parable clearly has wide-ranging religious implications. It would certainly refuse any use of religious symbolism to divide people and to create enemies. Christians must certainly accept the parable as a call to treat all as neighbors. Such demands are always difficult for any human community and they have been so throughout the history of Christianity. More than that, this parable suggests that compassion can transform such deeply engrained prejudices as those at issue in the story. The prevailing pessimism about human aggression and hostility cannot be shared by anyone who accepts this parable as a vision of what is possible—however unusual.

We have seen that the original audience would have found themselves faced with something of a challenge. They would have to identify with the victim in such a way that the Samaritan's action not only provides relief but challenges their own convictions of personal or moral superiority to those considered as enemies. Religious symbols are not aimed at making us superior to others but at bringing us to the position of recognizing the equality or even superiority of the persons we might have treated as inferior. There are many examples of such challenges in Jesus' own ministry. Such a perspective would no longer engage in the kind of judging others or angry retaliation against which Jesus speaks. Indeed the Jewish audience finds that its very survival depends not upon its own actions but upon the enemy's exemplification of the highest possible degree of compassion. Most people would not have high expectations of their enemies in such a situation. Yet such a story does more for our appreciation of what is at stake in the commandments of love of neighbor and enemy than all the repetition of the commandments and legal definition in the world. It challenges the imagination to consider the possibility that one might be "safe" as a helpless victim in the encounter with the enemy. It also suggests that the kind of fostering of peace between peoples that most of the great world religions profess really demands such an imaginative re-orientation of the expectations of believers. God's rule over cre-ation is such that the world is not trapped in endless cycles of violence and retaliation but a cycle that can be broken when people recognize their own control over the dynamics of enmity. Nothing obliges the Samaritan to respond to the Jew as an en-emy, and indeed he does not do so. One of the most important functions of religious reconciliation is to enable people to break out of similar cycles of violence and hatred. The enemy does not have to be an enemy. The so-called enemy to whom you secretly think you are superior may not be so inferior either. Perhaps he or she will even show you an unsurpassed lesson about the truth of love and compassion.

Unmerciful Servant (Mt 18:23–35)

The Good Samaritan left the audience with a question: What did the victim do? Did his approach to the Samaritan change after the experience? The parable of the Unmerciful Servant makes it clear that though such experiences are intended to change the way in which we deal with others, Jesus recognizes that they do not always have such an effect. Matthew uses the parable to conclude a discourse on relations between Christians. It illustrates the forgiveness that should be part of all disputes within the community. Thus it serves as an example of love of neighbor, that is, a member of one's own community. Like the Good Samaritan, this parable has been attached to a legal ex-change. Peter tries to get Jesus to make a legal determination of how many times one is required to forgive a fellow Christian who has wronged one. Jesus brushes aside Peter's quite generous "seven?" with an expression that means as many as necessary (Mt 18:21–22). This parable follows. As would be expected, Mat-thew has heightened the references to judgment in this parable to serve as a warning to Christians (vv. 34f).

Historical Background

Some features of the story do not suit everyday life under Jewish Law. A man's wife and children would not have been sold into slavery to pay a debt. The initial debt of 10,000 talents would be like saying "several billion." The annual income from Herod the Great's whole kingdom is only reported at 900 talents. Obviously, no individual could owe such a debt. These elements in the parable suggest that the story is dealing with what people imagined the kings of the time to be like. The first servant is pictured as an official under one of the fabulously wealthy kings of the east. The debt would have been incurred as part of his service. Perhaps he is in charge of collecting taxes in part of the king's empire. The sum involved need not be realistic. The story simply represents what people imagined the great kings of Egypt or Persia to have been like.

Literary Analysis

The story is arranged in alternating scenes. Direct discourse points to the stages in which successive reckoning takes place. The initial threat to sell the man and his family into slavery—while quite a change for a high official in such a court—would not, of course, repay the debt. It simply serves as an indication that the servant has no further resources left to deal with the situation. The two requests for forgiveness are presented in parallel scenes. The requests are made in identical wording.

	KING-SERVANT	SERVANT-SERVANT
amount owed	10,000 talents	100 denarii
expressed anger	sell man and family	seize throat
request for time	"have patience with me and I will repay you all"	"have patience with me and I will repay you"
response	having pity released forgave debt	—— refused had imprisoned until pays what he owes

The expressions "owe, repay, servant" carry through these two scenes to the final reckoning between the king and the servant. There, the additional expressions "fellow servant" and "mercy" are introduced. The conclusion in v. 34 makes the fate of the first parallel with what he had done to his fellow servant. The wording is not quite identical. It may have been added to facilitate the transition to the judgment application that Matthew gives in v. 35. The original might have ended with the question. The audience would supply some judgment; perhaps they would assume that the king would carry through his original threat. For this man there is no chance that what he owed could have been paid, of course.

The structure of the plot is clear enough. What could have been a situation of unparalleled good fortune is turned to nothing, since it has no effect on the servant's behavior toward his fellow servant. He has just been forgiven a debt he could never have been expected to repay only to refuse to grant the other man time to repay a debt that one might easily expect him to make good on. The conclusion focuses attention on the incongruity between the two actions. The king's action in forgiving the huge debt is all the more incredulous when one remembers that Jews commonly saw such kings as examples of the height of inhumanity. The same verb is used to describe the king's reason for forgiving the large debt, *splanchnein,* as was used in the Good Samaritan to explain the Samaritan's assistance. Just as a Samaritan could never be expected to aid a Jew, so such an oriental potentate could never be expected to show mercy to a vastly inferior servant—especially one who had clearly failed so miserably in delivering the large sum such kings were known to extract from their subjects. But that glorious surprise is quickly reversed. Though the same words of appeal are used (with the slight irony that every time the debt of the first servant is mentioned he promises or is required to pay *everything/all*—an obviously impossible promise), he cannot recognize the same appeal from which he has just benefited. The words do not awaken any compassion in him. He would not even have had to forgive the debt; he only had to grant the second servant more time to pay! Thus, he not only fails the larger test of generosity but even the lesser one of allowing an extension on the obligation.

Teaching of Jesus

This parable has more of the shape of a folktale than those which refer to situations that the audience is likely to encounter in everyday life. Yet the association between forgiveness and one's stance vis-à-vis God that belongs to the Matthean context is also found in the wisdom tradition as we have seen. Mt 5:42 also contains a saying about lending to the person who wishes to borrow. The parable might have been associated with the general question of forgiveness or it might have been a further illustration of the teaching on non-retaliation. One does not need to allegorize the king as God in order to see the point of the parable. It plays upon imaginative presuppositions about great kings and their behavior in order to present an image of how foolish our demands for the exact letter of the law really are. At the same time, the parable presents a possibility that was left hanging at the end of the parable of the Good Samaritan. Perhaps a person would not be touched by the experience at all. Thus, despite the "fantasy" side to the story, the parable acknowledges a reality of human life that the striking examples of compassion in the Samaritan and the king of this parable might seem to ignore. There are those who are not moved to compassion even when they have just experienced it themselves, and even when the appeal is made to their compassion in the very same words. This parable suggests that Jesus did not consider "love of enemies/neighbor" as a piece of unrealistic magic. An experience of such compassion should certainly—but well might not change the person who is the object of it.

Human Significance

This last observation points to an element of human significance that is often overlooked in the interpretation of this parable. The Matthean context is a clue to the importance of such a recognition. Peter is concerned about how often he must forgive a fellow Christian who has wronged him. On the idealistic view of forgiveness, one might assume that the offender would not repeat the offense—or at least certainly not more than the seven times Peter suggests—since he or she would be "reformed" by the experience of forgiveness. Jesus refuses to set any limit to the number of times the person might be forgiven. This parable is an indication for the Christian in Peter's position of why not. People are not necessarily changed by experiences of forgiveness—even one so "unimaginable" as this. At the same time, the story makes it clear that failure to change is not "all right." It is an offense against the extraordinary compassion one has received.

You might say that one reason the servant is not changed is his inability to make the connection between what has happened to him and what he should do for others. Remember that the ancient philosophers advised kings that "love of enemies" might be in one's best interest if it created a loyal ally. The servant might well have had such a reaction toward the king and been willing, even eager to repay him in the future. What he does not recognize is that his obligation is toward others. Students in whom one has invested a lot of extra time are always wishing they could do something to repay that investment of time and energy. They are often surprised when I tell them that I am not the one they are to repay. They will have their opportunity to help other people somewhere along the line, just as my helping them is really repaying a debt that I owe to many people who took extra time and trouble with me. In other words, we make the mistake of thinking that such obligations are like debts, simply reciprocal relationships between the two parties involved. The servant owes the king everything for his compassion but he does not owe the rest of the world anything. Instead, we need to recognize that such obligations are transitive from one person to another and so on. We cannot repay those who take such time and trouble with us; we cannot often repay the people who give us the break that makes all the difference in our lives; we cannot really repay our parents. But all of those investments of time and energy are not intended simply to be a one-to-one, closed relationship. They are intended to help us become the kind of people who can do the same for another person somewhere down the line. Failure to recognize that important aspect of our relationships with each other will certainly contribute to the inability to perceive situations in which we are called upon to show the same concern, compassion or whatever that was shown to us.

Religious Significance

These reflections make some sense of the claim that God's forgiveness of us and our forgiveness of others are related. Most of us are brought up with that as a moral injunction. Most of us probably picture God as so superior—like the great oriental potentate—that while we recognize the required gratitude in theory, it seems to us that "he can afford it" and we find it difficult to be touched by the experience in a way that changes our action toward others. The simple version of part of the Unmerciful Servant in Lk 7:41–43, the Two Debtors, is as far as we get. This proverb-style parable simply asserts that the one who is forgiven much loves much, while lesser forgiveness indicates less love. This parable recognizes that such conclusions do not get at the heart of the issue. They only apply to reciprocal relationships— and even there our proverbial wisdom may find itself strained. In fact, God's forgiveness of us is not primarily concerned with getting himself loved, a two-party reciprocal relationship. The parable is not meant to imply that I have some set of obligations to God, that I have to pay off in certain types of behavior toward others. Rather, it suggests that the experiences we have of compassion, forgiveness, mercy, extra assistance, and so on are meant to be directed outward. They are not relationships to be shaped solely on the legal model in which the contract says that I owe you or you owe me something under certain conditions, and if you fail to perform, I can execute certain legal claims against you. The king's compassionate forgiveness had not laid any legal claim on the servant, but it should have presented him with a personal one. It should have changed his own behavior in similar situations and did not. Unlike the instances of conqueror and client king, treated by the ancient philosophers, this king had nothing to gain by his action. Perhaps the man would be a loyal servant, but he would not provide a needed ally—as the Romans had done when Augustus restored Herod the Great's kingdom even though Herod had been the ally of his enemy. Thus, in its way this parable is as incredible as that of the Good Samaritan. Compassion is the only reason for the extraordinary action taken by the king. Similarly, divine forgiveness is like that. It is between parties who are so unequal that there is "no reason," no obligation that can be created and fulfilled. It must be applied in transitive fashion to other relationships.

Schottroff [12] suggests that the parable has theological implications as applied to the disciples. Its aim is to guide their response to situations of hostility. If they respond in a non-retaliatory fashion, then their opponents may still be converted. If, on the other hand, they treat the opponent as enemy, the cycle of violence will be continued. However, the "love command" does not transform such situations automatically. In this parable, the person one would least expect to show pity, the great king, behaves in an extraordinary way. The servant, who could well take the requested action, turns around and insists on the letter of the law. The hostility that the disciple encounters does not release him or her from the obligation to love. Nor is it an indication that the love of neighbor/enemy is powerless to transform relationships based on violence and aggression.

People often object that Jesus' teaching about the love of neighbor/enemy would put a person at a disadvantage in a world where aggression is barely controlled by societal restraints of law and force. Sigmund Freud concludes his *Civilization and Its Discontents* with this psychological evaluation of the love command:

> The command to love our neighbors is the strongest defense against human aggressiveness and it is a superlative example of the unpsychological attitude of the cultural super-ego. The command is impossible to fulfill; such an enormous inflation of love can only lower its value and not remedy the evil. . . . Anyone who follows such preaching in the present state of civilization only puts himself at a disadvantage beside all those who set it at naught.

Freud's analysis raises three issues. First, civilization depends upon our ability to control and moderate aggressive instincts. Cultural need has generated the love command as an expression of that necessity. If it were indeed possible for all members of a society to internalize this command, then the problem might well be solved. Second, any realistic appraisal of human psychic life would, in Freud's opinion, have to admit that it is not possible to expand love to that degree. Love is of its nature attached to selective objects. Third, such a person would be at a severe disadvantage in a society which plays by other rules. The second objection is perhaps the easiest to deal with. Love, in the sense of the love command, does not require the orientation of feeling around the neighbor as object that characterizes what we speak of as love. As all the examples of the command in philosophical, Jewish and Christian traditions show, the issue is how I treat the neighbor, not how I feel toward him or her. It is certainly possible for me to make decisions on how I will treat another person according to the norm that I would apply to a person that I did love—the Good Samaritan does exactly that. Freud's account of the psychological origins of such a commandment, the first point, might be said to be an explanation of how such teaching comes to appear in a variety of religious traditions—not only Judaism and Christianity. Humans have always recognized that religion must deal with human aggression and the consequent suffering that arises from it. They are quite capable of recognizing that the alternative to such a situation would be one in which the neighbor were the object of one's love or compassion.

As an ideal, then, the love command reflects an important truth about human beings and their relationships. They are fraught with aggression and hostility, which our legal arrangements can only partially control. At the same time, humans are unwilling to suppose that such precarious arrangements are the final truth of our social interaction. Love and family relationships provide models that suggest the possibility of an alternative more broadly applied: all members of the group or all humans may be considered as "family." So considered, they may be treated with a compassion or indulgence or forgiveness that we would not extend to outsiders or enemies. The problem comes with the question of real action. Is Freud right that the commandment as expressed represents an impossibility? Does it set one at a disadvantage in the real, human world of conflict, legal relationships and aggression?

Presented with the love command in the abstract, most people would certainly agree. The first thing to be noticed about the parables in which it is given expression is that it is not presented as a real disadvantage for the persons who show the extraordinary compassion required. The Samaritan would appear to be a well-off merchant of some kind who is traveling on an accustomed route. He has the means—and the standing with the innkeeper—to provide for the victim. Whatever the king does to the servant, he is not going to recover the 10,000 talents in tribute. If he requires that he will have to take some other means to get it. The price brought by the sale of the man and his family would be negligible to such a king. It merely represents a horrible punishment for the servant—and perhaps a warning to other servants who might be lax in such obligations. The servant himself could have extended time to the fellow servant without necessarily losing the sum of money at issue. Similarly the context within which Matthew sets the parable of the Unforgiving Servant presents a very specific issue: How often does one forgive a fellow member of the community? The proposal of "seven times," which Jesus rejects, itself suggests that the forgiveness is not something that will put the person involved at a disadvantage. Further, all of the stories and their contexts acknowledge the fact that the world as humans experience it does not fall into such a neat pattern that legal processes and even punishment can always be abolished. Rather, the stories suggest that compassion, forgiveness, love of neighbor and even love of enemy are possible in certain concrete situations. The Samaritan is picking up a Jewish victim after all, not a fully armed soldier. These are situations in which the party extending compassion has more than enough resources to respond to the need of another person who is trapped in an impossible situation. The benefactor does not suffer any loss through his or her action any more than such a person would feel deprived by extending aid to a close friend or a family member. Thus, the parables suggest the context in which the extraordinary sounding ideal may fit quite appropriately into the world of human relationships, not one that is either psychologically unrealistic or designed to reduce the disciple to a permanent status as a victim.

Summary

We have seen that the love command is represented as the ideal fulfillment of the law in other religious traditions. Indeed, it expresses some of the deepest aspirations of humanity, since it sets forth the real condition for the justice and peace that humans find so sadly lacking in their world. Law, force and conquest may provide uneasy solutions, but they do not transform the relationships that can be the source of violence in the future. The stories of the love command suggest that even the most unlikely situations may be transformed if compassion brings about a new understanding for the other person, an understanding which does not insist on the categories friend-enemy or king-servant. They do not presuppose that such transformations are either automatic or easy to accept. They may even be quite unrecognized by one of the parties involved. But they also suggest that this is no false ideal of behavior, or projection of the cultural super-ego. It is a possible experience in many of the interactions of our life, one which may be the real source of hope for the violence and enmity which seems to be taken for granted as "the way life is." Jesus insists that it does not have to be that way or that we have to be a victim. Compassion and forgiveness are the expression of the rule of God precisely in a world marred by inequality, enmity and victimization.

STUDY QUESTIONS

1. Give two examples of Jewish use of the love command.

2. What are the two forms of the love command?

3. Give two examples of how the love command would be interpreted in ancient society.

4. Write a short dialogue between the Jewish man and the Samaritan at the inn two days later. What do you think the Jewish man told his friends about the incident when he finally returned home?

5. Pick a modern situation of social or racial hatred. How do you think Jesus' teaching about love could be applied in that situation?

6. Why do you think the unmerciful servant failed to grant his fellow servant's request? Can you think of any modern examples of such refusal to show mercy by a person who has received it?

7. How do you respond to the claim that the love command is unrealistic? Why?

Chapter Nine

REVERSAL, EQUALITY AND REWARD

The discussion of the love commandment in the previous chapter showed that there is a certain discrepancy between what is legally permissible and what is an expression of love for the neighbor. Some have gone so far as to suggest that Jesus' teaching would undermine the foundations of law, punishment and reward that are necessary for any viable social order. The fate of the Unforgiving Servant indicates that early Christians did not necessarily find such teaching in the parables. On the other hand, the constant reminders of judgment in the Matthean narrative suggest that at least some members of his community had taken the expressions of gracious forgiveness and salvation for sinners in Christianity to mean that righteous action was not a requirement for discipleship. They may have thought that as Christians they were already beyond judgment. The parables constantly challenge our limited judgments about who is good, compassionate, and forgiving and who is not. These challenges are expressed by some surprising reversals in plot. Is it possible to have judgment along with such compassion? Or have all the elements of judgment been added by Christians unable to live in the face of such radical expressions of divine forgiveness?

Reversal in the Parables

The longer narrative parables typically present unexpected twists in plot. The most unusual people wind up as beneficiaries of the circumstances set up by the story:

(a) The prodigal son is treated as "successful son returning home."
(b) Outcasts become the guests of the wealthy man at a feast.
(c) The enemy (Samaritan) is the one who saves your (Jewish) life.
(d) An oriental potentate is compassionate beyond measure to a slave.

Less startling are the negative reversals in which the characters who "don't deserve it" are turned out:

(a) The improperly attired guest is cast out of the wedding.
(b) The negligent servants (virgins) are excluded from the wedding.
(c) The rich man, who neglected the Torah, is in hell.
(d) The guests with other concerns exclude themselves from the feast.

Some interpreters speak of reversal as the defining characteristic of Jesus' use of the parable. Parables fit into the larger context of his attack on the boundaries and classifications that we have set up. These categorizations often stand in the way of our appreciation of the presence and purposes of God [e.g. Crossan, 1975:55–60; 1976:93–110, who argues that while myths establish the order of the world, parables upset it]. Thus, the parables serve as foundation language for a renewal of faith. Such renewal requires the ability to turn around what everyone takes for granted about God and religion [see Funk, 1975:64f].

However, reversal should not be interpreted as twentieth century glorying in paradox [see the well-taken objections of Beardslee:156–159]. Jesus' use of the wisdom traditions and his allusions to the Old Testament show that the parabolic reversal is presented within the context of a securely established tradition. They remind us that what is perceived as true righteous-

ness is grounded in God's intention for his creation (ibid.:170f).
Modern fascination with the paradoxical, on the other hand, mirrors a world in which the certain traditions have fallen apart, a
world in which some hope to be able to live through its very paradox.

We have seen that much of the reversal in the parables is
presented in a comic vein. These are not the great reversals of
tragic plots. All around us we find that the types for Jesus' stories—anonymous, self-absorbed guests, indulgent and stupid rich
people, negligent servants—can be cast easily enough from our
own experience as can prodigal sons and elder, jealous but dutiful brothers. Thus, the comic becomes a way of looking at ourselves in "low relief." There is no part of our life that cannot
appear comic when approached from the right angle, frequently
by simply exaggerating one feature of common situations. The
comic loosens the hold that the solemnity of the world and our
socio-cultural arrangements have on us. In so doing, we are able
to live with its anomalies, inequities and absurdities. Sometimes
the comic appears as the only mode of survival in hopeless situations. The comic presentation of life is hardly trivial. Critic
Walter Kerr calls it "the groan made gay" [*Tragedy and Comedy*:19]. For Jesus, the comic dimensions of the parables are part
of the renewal of faith that is able to discern God's presence and
action in areas of the world that would hardly dignify themselves
with such claims. In contrast, there is no comedy in the great,
apocalyptic visions of world judgment; the stakes are too high.
Yet the Rich Man and Lazarus can even turn such scenes to the
comic when focused on a single individual rather than the whole
of human history.

The comic dimensions of reversal in the parables show that
Jesus is not out to destroy the fundamental moral truths of his
tradition any more than a political satire is out to destroy our
government. Comic reversals break down the barriers that the
solemnity of social and religious convention may erect between
us and those realities. They are important in Jesus' approach to
the sinners and outcasts, since they can "defuse" the feeling of
alienation that is often created by the official presentations of
righteousness. Such alienation may represent an emotional bar-
rier to the grace of God which Jesus proclaims as present. We
have to recognize that comic resolution of a plot thrives on a kind
of exaggeration and "injustice" that we would find intolerable as

a regular policy in real life. They produce equality by bringing the high and mighty down to the level of the lowly or exalting the lowly to a mock status with the lofty. Jesus is constantly playing with the leveling effect of comic reversal because the equality in which we all stand before God is fundamental to his message. There is no justification for the boundaries which we set up between ourselves and others. (If you have seen the play or the movie "Godspell," you have seen some brilliant presentations of the comic dimensions of the parables in fantasy and mime.)

Both the "happy" and the "sad" endings to a character's fate are presented in the comic vein as we have seen. At the same time the shifts in fate do not get out of hand. We are guaranteed that the really "bad guys" are held responsible for their actions. We are still responsible for the predicaments which we get ourselves into. The comic also thrives on an element of surprise. What we expect to happen according to the logic of our everyday world would hardly make a funny story. That element of surprise is important in Jesus' presentation of God's presence and grace as breaking into the everyday world of his audience. It is not limited to solemn occasions or persons. We cannot program compassion from others. God takes his own initiative in his own time. We have no claims on him by which we can insist on specific blessings for ourselves or vengeance for others—as unfortunate consequence of some forms of apocalyptic preaching.

The comic reversal makes it possible to present the judgment of some characters without the vengeance or resentment that is sometimes found in other writings of the period. The Rich Man is rather pathetic; he is certainly punished, but he is not the object of vengeful gloating. Though they may not succeed, the parables leave the way open for reconciliation between opposing groups. The rich may still belong to this community; so may elder brothers. In the case of the elder brother, the feelings of "the righteous" are acknowledged as not without importance even if Jesus is going to insist on the propriety of the reception given to the prodigal son. Thus, the parables constantly present characters who escape the dualistic division of humanity into wicked/ righteous that dominates apocalyptic preaching. Such realism accords better with the world that most of us experience. That is the world in which they seek to inspire new patterns of behavior. While some parables present pictures of judgment, others present an equality of reward—even undeserved generosity as in the case of the prodigal son. Recognition of God's rule seems to require a world in which both can be true.

Vineyard Workers (Mt 20:1–16)

This parable will hardly be a favorite with those who insist that all rewards be parceled out according to a strict system of justice. The elder brothers of the world have a difficult time with stories such as this one. Matthew has taken v. 16 from 19:30 to form an inclusio with the previous section and to set this parable off from the passion prediction which comes after it. Associating the parable with what comes before makes it an answer to the question about the rewards for those who follow Jesus (19:27). Jesus' immediate answer might lead one to think that reward was a matter of careful calculation. The twelve are to sit on thrones judging the tribes of Israel while others are rewarded one hundredfold for everything that they have left in following Jesus. This parable defends God's freedom in rewarding all. It can also be read in light of the coming dispute caused by the sons of Zebedee who want special places at the right and left hand of Jesus. The reader will already recognize the absurdity of such a request [Meier:141].

Unlike the statement about a hundredfold reward for whatever one has given up, this story does not present the usual eschatological reversal. Rather, a peculiar reversal in order of pay leads those who had worked all day to find out what the others have received. Crossan argues that vv. 14f were also added by Matthew since they draw out the point of the story and put the owner in the unusual posture of justifying himself. Verse 14 introduces the phrase "last" from the eschatological application in v. 16. The language of v. 15b also seems most suited to such a context—literally, "Or is your eye evil because I am good?" The dichotomy wicked/good is typical of judgment language but not required by the story itself or the grumbling of those who had worked all day. (They are no different than the elder brother in the Prodigal Son.) [See Crossan, 1973:111–113] Though the language may have been influenced by the application of the parable to judgment, one might as well argue that self-justification is exactly what one would expect. Such behavior is appropriate to the human situation—and is somewhat paralleled in the dia-

logue exchange with the elder son in the Prodigal Son. The owner is angry over the resentment that his action has provoked. He
is not, after all, a direct image of God, though the story as a
whole may be taken as an example of how the divine undergirds
life [Breech:35f]. Unlike the reversals presupposed in eschatological judgment scenes, this story has only a partial reversal.
The people who worked all day receive exactly what they had
agreed to; those who worked only an hour received something
they never could have expected.

Literary Analysis

One of the key questions for a literary analysis of this story
is the issue of its focus. Is it primarily the story of divine generosity as exemplified in the extraordinary wage paid the last
group [so Dodd:94]? If so, then Crossan is right and v. 13 would
be a sufficient ending. Or is it like the Prodigal Son, a story that
seeks to reconcile the "all day" workers who have received only
what is due them to the extraordinarily generous gift made to
the others? Like the Prodigal Son, we never know what they did
in response to the owner's answer. Jeremias points out that this
parable is not one of divine mercy when viewed from their perspective. They only receive what was a standard day's wage. Giv-
en the economic fluctuations in Galilee, that might be adequate
or it might represent as little as a fourth of what would be required to get by. It is not anything out of the usual in any case.
Jeremias thinks that like the Prodigal Son this parable really focuses on the "all day" workers and is aimed at those critical of
Jesus' acceptance of outcasts and sinners.

Much of the story is in direct discourse:

    I. ND, vv. 1f: setting up the situation. A man is out hiring
       vineyard workers for the usual wage.

   II. DD, vv. 3f: the second group hired agreeing to work for
       what is fair/just. The reader would assume that the
       same arrangement applies to the rest of the groups that
       are hired.

  III. ND, vv. 5f: hiring of further groups of workers. Notice
       that the narrative is punctuated with the words "com-
       ing out of the vineyard, standing idle, going (into the
       vineyard)." The situation is typical of the chronic un-

employment of the time. No one would be surprised at laborers standing all day without work.

IV. DD, v. 6f: hiring of the final group. The exchange between the owner and this last group does not provide any information that would have been unknown to the audience. Nor does it imply some fault on the part of the workers who still had no work. The two dialogue sections in the first half of the story call attention to two realities in the life of a day laborer: the day's wage and the chronic underemployment, which meant that one might well pass a day without even that. They have no control over what the terms are. Hence, the other groups are quite happy to work for "what is just." This last group would have seen this man coming and others going into his vineyard all day. They would probably not even expect work at such a late hour. The dialogue serves to set up contact between the two groups. These workers would certainly have been surprised and pleased to receive something for the day. In such an economy, a day in which everyone in the market managed to have some sort of work would in itself be cause for rejoicing.

V. DD, v. 8: instructions to the steward to pay the wages beginning with the last. Before the audience can dwell on the unusual circumstances, the paying of wages begins. The order is reversed so as to set up the confrontation between the owner and the group that had worked all day.

VI. ND, vv. 9f: payment of the wages. A new set of terms link this section with what follows "last/first." the section is tied with what has preceded by the expressions "single denarius," "hour," "hired," "coming" (to receive pay as the reversal of going into the vineyard to work). There is no mention of paying the intervening groups explicitly. Their function in the story was twofold. The conditions under which the third hour group was hired set up the expectation that each group would be paid according to the amount of time worked. Second, the repetitive trips to hire more laborers filled out the day between the first and last group and made it clear how late they really were in being hired.

VII. DD, vv. 11–15: discussion of the wages actually paid.
Many of the words in this section are picked up from
the rest of the story: "first/last," "hour," "day," "make
an agreement," "denarius," "go." The motif of "what is
just" from v. 3 recurs in v. 13: the owner did no "injustice" to the first group, since he honored the agreement
between them. Verses 14f introduce a further contrast,
"what is yours" (= day's wage) and "what is mine"
(owner's wealth). This contrast is another reminder of
the economic conditions that are reflected in this parable.

A number of verbal parallels to earlier materials make the
actual complaint of those who had worked all day stand out in
sharp focus: "these last worked *(poiein)* one hour, and you have
made *(poiein)* them equal to us—to the ones who bore the burden
of the day and the heat." As in the Prodigal Son, the owner's response will not deny that the facts are as these workers present
them. He appeals to the legal agreement between himself and
the workers as the father did. But unlike the father in that story,
the owner refuses to give any justification for his behavior toward the group that worked only one hour.

The story revolves around what is fair/just, since that is the
agreement made between the owner and the laborers: the accusation leveled by the ones who had worked all day, and the substance of the owner's defense. He insists that he had not been
unjust *(adikos)* to them, since he has fulfilled the terms of their
contract. They claim, on the other hand, that making one hour
equal to those who have worked all day is unfair. We have no
hint of how the workers would have responded to the owner's response. One suspects that their hard feelings would have persist-
ed and perhaps even poisoned their relationship with the
workers who had received the unusual benefit of a day's wage.
Remember that they will all be back together in the marketplace
waiting for work on the next day. Sometime the same owner will
also be back looking for people to work in his vineyard. But with
the situation of unemployment as grave as that portrayed in this
parable, one suspects that he will not have any trouble finding
people willing to work no matter what his reputation is. Verse
15b moralizes the tale somewhat by casting the grumbling workers in a bad light in contrast to the goodness of the owner. It

serves as a culmination of the series of rhetorical questions which begins in v. 14b. This series of questions reinforces the difference between the day laborers and such owners. The owners can do what they please with their money. His harsh rebuke of the grumbling workers represents the realities of life in such a situation.

The story does not imply that peace and harmony is established. Nor is it a celebration of overwhelming generosity. No group receives more than the minimum day's wage. Though such behavior is somewhat unusual, especially as the owner shows himself to be the rather usual harsh master insisting upon his position and rights in his exchange with the first group, it is not beyond the realm of possibility. Notice that no motivation is given for his action beyond the self-justification at the end that he is "good." Unlike the stories which deal with the love command, compassion is not introduced as a motivating factor prior to the action. Perhaps it is best to regard this story as a photo, an image of how humans actually behave, rather than as a tragic or comic plot. The last group of workers only figure in the story insofar as their pay provokes the confrontation between the owner and the first group. The first group of workers have at the end of the story exactly what they had contracted for in the beginning. They would have been satisfied with that if it had not been for the treatment given the group that only worked an hour. The contrast is what makes them angry and jealous. Though that attitude is rejected, and though it gains them nothing, they have not lost anything.

Historical Background

The economic situation appears straightforward enough. We have already dealt with the realities of underemployment in villages in assessing the plot. It is as important to avoid important moral judgments against those workers who have not been hired at the last hour as it is to avoid explaining the master's action or the grumbling of the first group in such a way as to condemn the sentiments expressed by the first group. Their feelings, like those expressed by the elder brother, are quite in line with the situation even though they have no legal complaint.

Jeremias looks to two first century A.D. Jewish apocalypses in which the issue of first/last appears in the context of the final judgment. These writings might indicate how the audience would have applied this story to the question of final judgment and reward. In IV Ezra 5, 42 the seer wants to know if previous generations are at a disadvantage when compared with those who survive until the judgment of the world. He is told, "I (=God) will make the judgment like a circle dance; the last there are not behind nor are the first in front." 2 Baruch 30, 2 says with reference to the general resurrection of the righteous that all souls will appear before the Messiah: "and a multitude of souls shall be seen together in one assemblage of one thought, and *the first shall rejoice* and *the last shall not be grieved.*" As far as the mysteries of the judgment go, the readers of these works are assured that the righteous will be rewarded in such a way that distinctions between first and last will not matter. All of them will be rejoicing together. Verse 16 might well be a proverbial summary of such sayings about the judgment as these. "First/last" and "last/first" are like the circle dance. It does not make any sense to ask such questions about the reward for the righteous. The situation is something like being at a party where there is so much food that even if all the guests ate non-stop, there would still be some left over. Even the younger children are less inclined to grab when they see more cookies and cake than they can possibly imagine consuming.

Teaching of Jesus

The parallels with the plot structure of the Prodigal Son suggest a context in which Jesus had to address the issue of the disaffection of the righteous. Somehow what is just has come to be felt as unjust when it means that all receive a minimum wage for varying amounts of work. Yet if Jeremias' suggestion as to the background of the "first/last" motif is correct, they must also have known that in the end a system of carefully graded rewards or concern with "when" a person lived in comparison to the end of the world is ridiculous. It is less clear whether this story could have been aimed at the disaffected. It certainly does not give much motivation for them to change their assessment of the owner. He honors his contract, but also appears as arbitrary and rather unfeeling. His response is certainly less sympathetic to their position than that of the father to the elder son. Perhaps the parable served more as an explanation for the disciples. They must have wondered at the resentment and hostility that also seemed to have been provoked by the teaching of Jesus. We often are too ready to blame that on hypocrisy on the side of the Pharisees or other pious people. These parables are less condemnatory. They present realistic, human images of how it is that what is fair, legally correct and so on can suddenly be felt to be grossly unfair. They do not accept the attitude engendered by that experience as appropriate to the situation, but they do acknowledge that some "good people" may feel compelled to object to what Jesus seems to be presenting as easy access to the rule of God. Also notice that they are never denied their "reward," just their complaint. Whatever they lose, they lose in their own feelings of hostility and resentment. But these feelings are not cause for their dramatic exclusion as in parables of judgment for failed action such as the Unforgiving Servant or the Foolish Virgins.

Human Significance

The emotions expressed in this story are common enough in many of our everyday experiences, whether it is trying to deal with a group of children who are afraid that one child's piece of cake is bigger than another's or with "all day" employees who feel that others are "getting by with murder" and yet still receiving the same wage. Anyone who has ever had to cope with such problems in a management situation knows how deep such hostilities can run, and also how angry one can get with the "complainers" even though one must acknowledge the legitimacy of their comparison. When promotions, raises, merit ratings, or grades come out, there are always some people who feel that they have to "soft pedal" their own success in order not to lose friends, as well as those who start crying: "Unfair!" Unless everyone is paid exactly the same, punching the same time clock and doing the same amount of work in the time allotted such feelings of unfairness seem inevitable. Many of our dealings with employees, students and children are taken up in moderating the situations that give rise to such distress so that some sort of harmony can be maintained in the community which is going to have to live, study or work together regardless of how these individuals feel about the matter.

We also know that if the principle of equality were exaggerated or announced in advance, the way in which people work might be significantly altered. A lawyer friend once surprised a group by commenting that even though he likes law, he would not be a lawyer if everyone were paid the same for working. Most of us in teaching, on the other hand, would continue what we are doing—perhaps because we know that we are paid significantly less than our friends in business and government and do not figure to lose in the trade-off. The people in Jesus' story do not have such options. As day-laborers they are at the bottom of the heap and pretty much have to accept whatever the owner decides to pay, as the story makes clear from the beginning. Both he and they know the score in that regard. Yet, even there they want a situation of strict distribution rather than a minimum day's wage for everyone. Human beings want a strict system of rewards—especially those who work all day or with the uncomplaining industry of the elder son. They will be easily outraged by behavior which favors those who do not seem to have earned what they receive.

Religious Significance

The parable may present a fairly accurate picture of the kind of reward structure humans consider "fair." Transfer of such a structure to the religious sphere can be quite misleading. The judgment of the righteous does not require that God reward each in strict numerical order and that he carefully weigh out the various accomplishments of each individual. The Matthean church had the additional problem of explaining how the Gentiles, who were now joining, could be included in equal salvation with Jewish Christians who had belonged to the people of God all along. This parable defends God's freedom to extend God's salvation to whomever he chooses.

I once had an African student, a convert to Christianity from the tribal religion of his ancestors, who became very irate when confronted with the idea that perhaps heaven was not arranged in carefully graded levels, and that God would more likely extend the same blissful salvation to all, whether it be a great apostle like Peter or some insignificant person who barely made it in among the righteous. He could not believe that a God could ignore all the demands of hierarchy and privilege that his own upbringing as a chief's son had taught him were part of the way the universe works. The other students in the class—mostly Protestant ministers from the U.S.—were equally amazed at the explosion over something they took to be an obvious fact of Christianity: that God loves and rewards all equally, even if some wind up working for him most of their lives while others only make it in in the last minute. Though this last does seem to be the position which Jesus himself defends, especially in his many injunctions against partiality and self-exaltation by those who are to be leaders in the community, the outburst voiced by my African student is probably more typical of the reaction that people in Jesus' time would have had. Ancient society was both traditional and rigidly hierarchical. Just as one assumed that the rich would have the best seats in the synagogue—something that Jas 2:1ff warns Christians against—so one might assume that the pious would have an equivalent advantage in the judgment. Jesus' parable challenges that view along with the social distinctions to which it had given rise.

If Luke had preserved the story, one suspects that he might have focused a little more strongly on the behavior of the owner as a model for Christian owners. He is presented as being "good" in his use of resources. The amount of work is not the issue in turning to the question of need. The community is to see that the poor among its members have the minimum needed to survive. The owner's behavior insures that everyone went home that day with the minimum amount needed for himself and his family. For some, that is what they earned exactly; for others that meant making them equal to those who had worked all day (anyone who became discouraged and left the marketplace early was out of luck). Though this picture of "what is just" does not quite fit our "work ethic" as enunciated by those who had worked all day, it does respond to other concerns that have been implicit in the ethical teaching of the Old Testament about the poor from the beginning. Sometimes it was presented as leaving grain in the field at reaping so that they could then come along and collect enough to live on. This man could be said to have come upon a variant of that old legislation. He has let those who were not hired by anyone come into the vineyard, do some work, and then receive a day's wage. Regardless of the outcry that might be raised by other groups, the people of God has an obligation to see that the minimum needs of those within the community are met. Remember that there were no public sources of welfare for such people. Thus the parable can be seen as a presentation of how the obligation to care for the poor might be met. It is not utopian. The owner does not cease to be a wealthy owner, free to do whatever he wishes. The laborers will all have to be back the next day. All it does is argue that justice requires a certain minimal concern for the poor. Such concern might be seen as particularly necessary in a situation of chronic underemployment. There is nothing unusual in some men standing idle because no one will hire them. One could even argue that the biblical insistence upon concern for the poor and helpless members of society comes down to asserting that the religious health of a society is directly indexed by its attention to such issues. This parable may be a vivid presentation of the issues, but it is also a fairly realistic expression of some of the human attitudes that might be evoked in certain attempts to meet them.

The Talents (Mt 25:14–30//Lk 19:12–27)

The previous parable by itself might seem to encourage another attitude: do the minimum possible to get the reward, since it will be the same for all. This parable will certainly explode such notions. Matthew's version belongs to the series of judgment parables with which he concludes Jesus' discourse teaching in the gospel. Not only are Christians to be warned against complacency; they must take care to increase what Jesus has given them. Verse 30 repeats the conclusion that Matthew added to the Wedding Garment. The Christian who fails to take these warnings to heart could find himself or herself excluded altogether. Matthew is concerned about the possibility that fear or "little faith" will keep people from true discipleship. The fear of the one talent servant serves as a warning against that attitude [Meier:176f].

The context in Luke is slightly different. The parable is introduced as part of a discussion about why the kingdom is delayed. The disciples are mistakenly expecting the kingdom to arrive when they reach Jerusalem (v. 12). Luke has combined this parable with another about a Throne Claimant (vv. 12, 14, 15a, 27). This insertion may not be a parable at all but a short recollection almost a century after the events of how Herod the Great came to the throne—much in the style of Luke's reference to the Roman census of 6 A.D. in 2:1 or the slaughter of the Galileans in 13:1. Herod had to go to Rome to enlist aid in gaining control of the kingdom which Augustus had bestowed upon him. The Jews sent a delegation to Rome to request that the Roman Senate not appoint Herod. Finally, Herod returned to take over his kingdom with aid from Roman troops. Certain economic and personal reversals among the local nobility followed his return to rule. Those who had been loyal to Herod in his absence received control of certain villages and farmlands in Galilee. Note that the rewards for the good servants, which are very general in Matthew, become *cities* in Luke (vv. 17b, 19b) under the influence of that incident [see Smith:141]. Thus the parable may have been combined with an historical memory about Herod's coming to power, since the structure of the two rewards was seen to be similar.

Several other elements in the Lukan version may also be secondary. Jewish law held that if your friend left money in your care while going on a journey and you went and buried it, then you were not liable if the money were lost. If you simply kept it hidden in your house, then you would have to repay him the sum if you were robbed. Matthew's fearful servant follows the letter of that law; Luke's does not—perhaps because that legal provision was not familiar to the audience. Luke has also increased the number of servants to ten, each of whom receives less than the talent of Matthew, but the conclusion preserves the 10–5–1 structure that we find in Matthew's version. Thus, Matthew's version seems to be a pretty fair representation of the basic parable and we may proceed to use it as text for our discussion of the parable.

Literary Analysis

The crisis points in the story are indicated by the exchanges that take place between the master and the servants.

I. ND, vv. 14–19: a rather lengthy narrative setting up the situation. It includes the master's departure and the actions of the servants. Since all these details are narrated, our attention is quickly brought to bear on the reckoning that occurs when he returns.

II. DD, vv. 20–23: episodes of reckoning with the two successful servants, both identically worded. Their success becomes formulaic. It is not the point at issue, though repetition of the story and the master's reward certainly heightens our concern about the third servant, since we know that he did not behave as the others did.

III. DD, vv. 24–28: reckoning with the one talent man. He shows that he is also apprehensive, since he begins making excuses before handing over the talent. His description of the master, "a hard man who reaps where he does not sow," suggests that the master is a merchant or businessman of some sort. Perhaps the journey was that of a merchant. In any event, it is clear that the servants knew that they were to invest the money. The law required them to hand over both the capital and profit to the master [McGaughy:242].

If the audience recognized the legal behavior of the third servant, they will also recognize that it is inappropriate to his situation as the servant of a hard master. That law was formulated to govern money given one friend by another for safekeeping. The master in this story is not giving money to his servants for safekeeping but so that they will look after his concerns while he is away. The third servant cannot hide his fear behind a law which does not apply to the situation. In addition, the hearer has already been presented with the examples of the two other servants who were entrusted with much more money and were able to handle it successfully. Thus, the plot seems clear enough. The tragedy is that the servant fails to take the risks required to increase his master's money. He would not even risk it with "the bankers"—not guaranteed as they are in our country—and let them take the risks as the master points out to him in v. 27. Thus, the tale may be said to turn on fear. This servant is so afraid of failure before this harsh master that he hopes to get by if he returns the talent even though he knows that that is not what his master really intended him to do with it. As the conclusion points out, what made him afraid of the master are the same things that make the policy he adopts to preserve himself absurd.

Historical Background

In addition to the legal features pertaining to money left with another, the image of a departing king entrusting valuables to others for safekeeping may have been part of popular folk wisdom. It is used to comfort a famous rabbi on the early death of his son:

> I will tell you a parable. What is this matter like? It is like a man with whom the king deposited something for safekeeping. Every day he wept and cried, "Alas, when shall I be free of responsibility for this deposit?" You, Rabbi, had a son. He studied the Scriptures, the Law, the Prophets, and the Writings, as well as the Mishnah—the Halakoth and the Haggadah. Then he departed the world sinless. Be comforted. You have given back what was entrusted to you intact. (Aboth R. Nathan, 14)

The application is typically rabbinic. The boy had studied the Scripture and the commentaries on it. He died without having sinned against the teaching of the Law. The analogy, called a "parable," suggests that there was probably a folk-saying about no anxiety being like that of a person to whom a king has entrusted something for safekeeping. The fear evidenced by the third servant might have been familiar to Jesus' audience from such a tradition.

McGaughy has ventured an even more sweeping suggestion for the origins of the motif of fear in this story. He suggests that fear of the Lord in post-exilic writings (like Job 23:13-17 and Ps 119:120) belonged to a picture of God as one who demands righteousness and yet seems to ignore the plight and suffering of his people. These passages reflect bitterness felt by some Jews who thought that they did not deserve the harsh punishment that God had laid on his people. Yet one still had to obey his commands. Some Jews may even have considered this apparent lack of concern on God's part a reason for only complying with the minimum requirements of the Law [McGaughy:244].

Teaching of Jesus

McGaughy's suggestion presupposes a rather direct allegorizing of the master as God, which is not typical of the parables of Jesus—particularly when the harsher sides of such masters are also presented as part of the dynamics of the story. However, the post-exilic wisdom traditions may have been behind the formulations of proverbs about "fear of the Lord" such as that which seems to be reflected in the rabbinic example. The dynamics of the story persuade the hearer that anyone who behaves like the third servant is bound to be headed for disaster. Perhaps Jesus himself told the story to address the issue of paralyzing fear in the face of a great mission. It also turns out that those who succeed are not thereby relieved of their responsibility. They will be put over greater things. There is no "safe" position. The only road to success is to take the risks of the first two servants. That is the only attitude which a disciple can take.

Human Significance

It is not difficult to translate this parable into our own lives. There are those who are so fearful of taking risks or being wrong that they never speak in a meeting until they are sure of what everyone thinks. They never take any initiative at work, or they become paralyzed by the fear of failure when presented with a promotion or job that would require such initiative. Students are so concerned for "good grades" that they will not take a difficult course or they constantly try to pester the teacher into telling them exactly what he or she wants even on assignments designed to test their own creativity and analytic abilities. Some people even go so far as to put themselves into situations which guarantee failure, since that is more secure than having tried and failed. Even the generalizing conclusion in Mt 25:29//Lk 19:16 can be said to be true of such people. They never gain anything because they never venture anything. People begin to suspect that they do not have any initiative or opinion of their own. We may also find ourselves in such situations when faced with new responsibilities. Everyone has to overcome some "fearfulness" when asked to venture into a new area. We may also use inappropriate tactics to avoid taking responsibility that we should assume, just as this fearful servant does. Instead, we have to recognize that the ability to take responsibility and risk is a vital part of our well-being and growth as humans. There is no point at which we can suddenly stop and say "no more" without losing something of our independence and creativity. Perhaps we also have to watch out for the hedges that we try to create to secure our own future. If they are as inappropriate as this man's was, then they may collapse on us in the end anyway.

Religious Significance

Discipleship clearly involves shouldering responsibility for what has been entrusted to us. Not everyone has the same amount entrusted to him or her, but everyone does have the responsibility for how he or she deals with what has been given. (The one hour laborers did have to work for their stipulated hour.) The apparent absence or indifference of God which had even led some to assume that this world was largely under the dominion of Satan cannot be invoked as an excuse for inaction, nor can fear of the consequences. We cannot ignore things that we know we ought to do as Christians—just as the fearful servant who "knew" what his master really wanted did.

Matthew's perspective has an additional dimension to the responsibility of Christians. They have been entrusted with seeing to the growth of Christianity in the world. We often think that the fate of Christianity in the world is someone else's business—perhaps that of the Pope, or priests, or ministers, or theologians, or religious educators, or some other group professionally identified with the concerns of the Christian Church. The parable suggests that all have some responsibility. We are not just charged with maintaining our faith in a kind of rear guard holding action that will get us through—barely. Actually, one has to see to its increase; that would seem to mean being able to hand that faith on to someone else. The question is raised as to whether or not our own faith is adult enough to engage in the dialogue that would be required to explain to someone who did not share our belief what that faith is all about. It also involves the risk of exposing ourselves and what we believe to the give and take of challenge by others. Such dialogue, challenge and open hostility were part of the experience of every Christian in the time of the evangelists. Matthew knows that it is essential for the well-being and spread of Christianity in the world that Christians be able to overcome their fears and speak openly about what they believe. When is the last time that you challenged one of the door to door preachers with your own faith?

Faithful Servant (Mt 24:45–51//Lk 12:42–46); Doorkeeper (Mk 13:33–37)

Several shorter parables about good/wicked servants rehearse the themes of the longer parables in simpler form. The master is away on a long journey. His absence either leads the servants to laxity, foolish or even outrageous behavior, or it inspires them to vigilance so that all is ready upon his return. The Doorkeeper appears in Mk 13 as part of the discourse about how the disciple is to regard the end of the world. Delay will not keep him or her from being prepared for the Lord's return. The beatitude form used to introduce the Faithful Servant suggests that that parable may have been derived from a proverb. It was then turned to a parable of judgment when attention focused on the surprise return and punishment of the evil servants. Matthew adds 24:51b to make it clear that the judgment does not demote the good servant but is the final judgment of God against all Christians who are unfaithful servants.

Summary

These parables raise a variety of issues around the biblical themes of faithful obedience and reward. They not only deal with the final reward expected by those faithful to God's word, but also with the various forms that their obedience/disobedience might take. God's vindication of all the righteous is certain; it does not require a carefully graded system of reward for first/last. But it also requires definite human obedience. There is no room for a minimal "holding action," nor is there cause for those who have worked longer and harder to compare themselves with others who have done less but nonetheless are accepted as servants. Similarly, we have to watch out for the assumptions that we make about what is just/fair. Perhaps there is another standard of need that is more important than the careful grading that we think is necessary. Is there some point at which we have to be concerned for the poor and border-line poor especially because there is not always a job for everyone willing to work on the open market? We also have a responsibility for our own faith. How well the message fares in the world is not someone else's business. A "holding action," no risk approach to religion will not work any better there than it will for a demanding boss. Ultimately, we have to be able to say that some part of the world is "better off" for our presence than it would have been without it. Lame duck or irrelevant excuses for why we have not ventured what even we know we should have will not hold water when held up to scrutiny. Most of the situations in the parables are familiar enough to us from our work, school, or general dealings with others. We often treat them more seriously on the human level than we do the religious issues raised by the preaching of Jesus. The judgment side of these parables reminds us that the religious dimensions of our lives are no less important even if we are not constantly being reminded by some grade report or job evaluation.

STUDY QUESTIONS

1. Give three examples of reversal in parables we have studied. What point is being made by the reversal in each case?

2. Try acting out one of the parables in such a way as to emphasize its comic dimensions. What feeling do you get from the story when you approach it in that light?

3. Write a dialogue between one of the first workers in the vineyard and one of the "one hour" men when they see each other in the marketplace the next day.

4. Can you think of a modern situation in which the vineyard owner's behavior might be a better approach than that advocated by the workers? What objections would have to be overcome?

5. What picture do we get from these parables about God as the one who judges and rewards? How is it different from human systems of punishment/reward?

6. What would you do if you felt like the one talent man? Why?

7. What do these parables and their interpretation by the evangelists suggest about the responsibilities of Christians?

Chapter Ten

ETHICS AND THE PARABLES

We have seen that the parables can take up rather complex issues of human behavior. They are not simple, one-line statements of ethical principles. In fact, their ability to reveal our varied motivations depends upon the story and not upon any single line of behavior that may be commended or rejected. The characters in these stories are not the ideals of obedience to the Torah that we find in some rabbinic examples; nor are they the opposite, the "wicked person." Most are somewhere in between, somewhere in the range of people that the audience either experienced as part of everyday life or—in the case of the king figures—imagined to act in certain ways. We see a wide range of human behavior, from the extraordinarily compassionate to laziness, to self-serving complaint and envy. The mirror images of life provided by the parables have led some to claim that they are not concerned with ethics at all. They argue that the teaching of Jesus never presents what by his audience would have been considered ethics, interpretation of the Law, proverbial teaching about the behavior of the wise person, or philosophic argument. "Ethics" is an abstraction we make from the portrayal of faith and the call to discipleship presented by Jesus [Perrin, 1967:109; Sanders, 1975:4–17].

Parables and the "Moral Mystery" of Humanity

No one can question the unusual style of much of the teaching of Jesus. To argue that that style prescinds from the larger question of ethics as it is formulated throughout the biblical tradition—how are humans to live in the presence of God, the creator and covenant partner of a people?—is dubious. Even if Jesus were to be making such an argument, which is unlikely, the audience hardly heard it as such. Further, there is no evidence that he deliberately intends to overturn the fundamental cast of the biblical pattern of discipleship—unless a person begins with that as an *a priori* and therefore rejects all later ethical interpretations and use of the wisdom tradition as so much accommodation by later Christians. His metaphors of the rule of God themselves imply that Jesus is entering this debate over what counts as righteousness before God.

Jesus does not enter this debate as an interpreter of the tradition in the manner of the Pharisees or as an apocalyptic visionary whose visions of judgment, bliss and punishment encourage the righteous to reject all the temptations to infidelity and wickedness with which they are surrounded. Instead, he appeals to the rule of God as in some way already present in the world in which humans live and as a source for their action. The parables challenge the hearer to make a choice as to how the story ought to go. Amos Wilder has spoken of them as presenting us with men in their "moral mystery." The issue is not so much principles of action but how people do in fact or can in fact behave in the circumstances that they find presented by life itself. Most lives do not fit the crisis dimensions of the textbook ethical problems; most may not even find themselves challenged by Pharisaic standards of obedience and righteousness. Those concerns require a certain education and devotion to study of the Scripture and its interpretation that the average villager would not have access to or time for. Such a person would just go along with the religious traditions and customs of the people with whom he or she lived, probably pretty much unchanged for centuries. Jesus' preaching addresses just such people. It does not require a technical language of philosophic analysis or scriptural learning. Many of the wisdom sayings would have been familiar. Certainly the characters and situations of the parables are well within the realm of imagination as possible if not actual occurrences. They suggest that God is just as much involved with the scale of village life as he is with the piety of the learned scribe or Pharisee or the cosmic destiny of nations. Notice that Jesus may be critical of the limitations that some of the other forms of piety had taken—especially when a certain elitism led the righteous to separate themselves from those who were not as observant—but he never turns the righteous into sinners. The vineyard workers would suggest that they will also be rewarded for their faithfulness by God. Jesus hopes that they can come to see what God is doing in calling the outcast of Israel through his ministry. Parables of reconciliation like the Prodigal Son may represent an attempt to bring those members of the audience into the same joyous community. But, even if the elder brother stays outside, he still remains with the father. The shepherd may spend more time on the lost sheep; the others do not need him. Thus, the righteous Jews who still found themselves opposed to Jesus' interpretation are not the faithless servants he condemns. Stories like the Good Samaritan go even further in challenging the absolute identification of the Law with righteousness. Anyone, even an enemy, may exemplify the compassion that is the fulfill ment of the Law. Outsiders are not sinners by definition. The dimensions of universal humanity presented by the parables of Jesus should also remind Christians that the righteousness imaged by Jesus is not limited to his followers. Anyone may act in such a way as to fulfill what the creator expects of his creatures. By the same token, failure to recognize the demands of such compassion may also be attributed to those who do not stand within the tradition of the Law. Certainly, the revelation in the Law was intended to guide humanity to righteousness before its creator. Jesus himself does not deny that Scripture is the revelation of God—though he often criticizes what humans have made of that Scripture. It does not take great acumen, or even acquaintance with the long history of failure and repentance on the part of God's people, to recognize that the Law often enough went unheard. The Rich Man should have heeded Moses on concern for the poor and did not.

Jesus' imaginative story-telling takes another approach. It presents the audience with the moral dimensions of the world that is all around them: villages, masters, slaves, vineyard owners, tenants, and day laborers, as well as the great kings, rich men, and potentates that most only imagined. The comic dimension of the stories brings all these people down to the level of the audience. Their actions and motivations are held up for our inspection and evaluation. Crossan suggests speaking of such an approach as fundamental morality. It is not concerned with specific dos and don'ts but with how we live our everyday lives in the presence of God, and what that presence means for the way in which we dwell with the other human persons in our surroundings and the situations in which we are to take action [Crossan, 1979:114–116]. The context of the parables and their allusions to great biblical themes make it clear that these stories are not optional vignettes, comic sketches to be observed and then forgotten. Their message is directed at the audience with the same seriousness as the messages of other such preachers. Another way of making the same point might be to say that the perspective on humans, their actions and their world presented in the parables coincides with the perspective on things taken by God himself.

This perspective is anything but distant and unconcerned about the realities of life for the "average" person. One could even argue that the small scale of God's concern for the least of his creatures makes it impossible to envisage the sweeping judgment and obliteration of "the evil ones" that some of the righteous considered the only solution to the dilemmas of the world in which they found themselves. Jesus rejects the image of the world as a hard place, so dominated by evil that the good can only prevail through heroic efforts on the part of the righteous. Any number of unlikely persons—Samaritans, Gentile kings—take extraordinary actions in these stories. They are compassionate beyond measure. Certainly, the world of the parables is a mixture of good and bad, faithful and faithless servants. But it comes out a pretty even mix. Those who are condemned in some way have usually excluded themselves through their own lack of perception, fear, or other negative behavior. They are not presented as living in a world that is stacked against them. Often other characters who take action appropriate to the situation show that both are open to a person. No person is unimportant regardless of his or her religious or social status. Such a vision does require that we be willing to shed some of our normal judgments and ways of classifying people. Forgiveness, perhaps even a foolish compassion, characterizes the relationship of the disciple with others. At the same time, some of the parables suggest that such extraordinary displays of forgiveness, generosity and compassion can still call out the negative and petty side of human behavior—envy, jealousy, self-aggrandizement.

These stories suggest that such negative dimensions can quite well be accommodated within the perspective of the kingdom. They are not evidence either against God or against the possibility of human righteousness. Such generous allowance for the failed sides of human behavior allows Jesus to present a face quite different from that of the stern moralism of the Pharisees. All groups get their say in these stories—the righteous elder brothers, all-day workers, the repentant, the lazy and the fearful. Whether comic or tinged with tragedy, that say is presented within a context of acceptance that allows one to see all facets of our human behavior—good and bad, adult and childish. Many of them can even be entertained with a certain good humor and affection unless they come to block all response to one's fellow man or woman or to God, like the servant who will try to avoid taking any risk with his talent or the rich man who may stumble over Lazarus at his door every day and still not give him a scrap to eat. There is a fearfulness, a blind self-indulgence, and a failure to respond to what is required of us for any number of other reasons that can exclude us from the final company of God. But that is a situation which is presented as regrettable and considerably less desirable than the inclusion of all. Thus Jesus has forged a picture of what it is to act out of the conviction that God does rule and is caring about all of his people. Such righteousness is to be as inclusive as possible. Anyone may attain its underlying compassion right in the circumstances of his or her life.

The Sheep and the Goats (Mt 25:31–46)

Matthew concludes his series of judgment parables with this heavily allegorized presentation of the judgment. Like the Ten Virgins, this parable is often considered a creation of the Matthean church. Like that parable, we can find behind Matthew's allegory many features that are characteristic of parables of Jesus. The play and movie "Godspell" have captured the comic aspect of this parable in mime. The sheep and the goats form a rather unruly flock, constantly straying toward the wrong side and shoved back into line by the herders. The comparison at the basis of the parable is that of a shepherd separating his flock. It has been combined with the early Christian preaching of Jesus as the glorious Son of Man to come in judgment on the whole earth. This combination is typical of the Q collection of Jesus' sayings and parables used by Matthew and Luke [see J. A. T. Robinson, 1962:76–92]. The original parable may also have made some use of Son of Man imagery [for the arguments in favor of Jesus' use of the Daniel motifs, see Moule, 1977:11–22]. Look up the passage in Dn 7:13ff where the suffering righteous of Israel are promised exaltation in the figure like a Son of Man who ascends to the divine throne.

Here is an example of the use of the Son of Man figure from the Enoch tradition which describes the final judgment:

There was great joy among them; they blessed, glorified and gave praise because the name of that Son of Man had been revealed to them. And he sat on the throne of his glory, and the sum of judgment was given to the Son of Man. He caused the sinners to pass away and be destroyed off the face of the earth, and those who have led the world astray. They will be bound with chains, and imprisoned in the gathering place of destruction, and all their works will vanish from the face of the earth. From that time on there will be nothing that is corruptible, for that Son of Man has appeared and has seated himself on the throne of his glory. All evil shall pass away from before him, and the word of that Son of Man shall go forth, and be strong before the Lord of Spirits (=God). (69:26–29)

Now imagine this glorious scene of judgment reduced to the problem of a shepherd separating sheep from goats. Any boy could do the job. There is none of the dramatic destruction of sinners. The language of such scenes is employed in the rather unusual context of sorting an unruly flock. No book of life or computer-assisted record of each person's deeds would be required to do this job. (The book of life, i.e. the righteous, is opened before God's throne in 1 En 47, 3f.) In fact, a good sheep dog would be of considerably more help than the angelic hosts.

Literary Analysis

Judgment scenes such as the one above are important for this parable, since it revises a traditional metaphor. The introduction of a flock of sheep and goats brings the whole down to the everyday scale so typical of Jesus' imagination. Most of the parable is taken up by the formally identical exchanges between the king and the representatives of the two groups. It exhibits the same peculiarity we noted in the Rich Man and Lazarus. The individuals being judged do not seem too bright. They do not seem to quite recognize that they are before the great throne of judgment. The Rich Man seemed rather obtuse in his attempts to get aid from Abraham. Here neither group seems too sure of what is going on. Even the sheep protest their salvation!

Their astonishment is found in the identification claimed between the glorious king and those in need. Identification of God and the poor can also be paralleled in rabbinic sources as Jeremias [207] points out:

> My children, when you give food to the poor, I counted
> it as though you had given it to me.
>
> (Mid. Tan. 15:9)

The list of deeds for which the sheep are rewarded is repeated four times in the last section almost like a litany. It reads like a list of the troubles that are to be reversed in the messianic age: food for the hungry, drink for the thirsty, hospitality for the stranger, clothing for the naked, aid for the sick and the imprisoned. The classic passage for such a list is Is 61:1–4, which is used as the opening of Jesus' ministry in Lk 4:18 and in the answer given to the disciples of John the Baptist in Mt 11:4. (Some interpreters also argue that it underlies one of the versions of the beatitudes.) Such actions were also considered to define "love of the brethren" in early Christian communities (e.g. Rom 12:9–21; 15:7; Jas 2:14–17; 5:14). Thus it seems that the list used at this point in the parable may reflect ethical instruction in early Christian communities. It may be a standard catechesis known to all members of the community. Certainly the repetition in the structure of the parable could easily lead the audience to join in by the third or fourth time around. It works on one's awareness when it is repeated verbally (in reading we may skip it as soon as we recognize that it is that list again), like a chant. Matthew then provides a formalized ending to indicate that this is the definitive statement about judgment (v. 46; see Meier, 1979:177).

The parable itself is more of an image of judgment than an actual story; consequently it is not appropriate to classify it according to plot. The combination of popular rhetoric about judgment as a great scene before the heavenly throne complete with the heavenly court and the book of life and a shepherd sorting the flock suggests that the popular image has gotten out of hand. There is no complicated reckoning to take place. All that is necessary is to sort the sheep from the goats. Even a small child can learn to tell the difference between the two types of animal and could accomplish the task. The second "surprise" appears in the contrast between the "king" image and the invisible outcasts with whom he is identified. They are so insignificant that even those who gave them the required assistance did not recognize the real import of what they were doing. Thus from a literary point of view, the parable is built on surprise contrasts. No one would imagine judgment to be like sorting sheep and goats. No one would conceive that helping a poor, unimportant person would have any relation to a king. The parable of the Rich Man and Lazarus gave us a good example of how invisible a poor person might be in society. Lazarus was just a bag of sores, lying at the door, being licked by the dogs—nothing more. In this tale, the poor, the hungry, the imprisoned, and the strangers are all fairly invisible even to those who did give them aid. They did not have to do so because they recognized that God's cause was identified with that of the poor.

Teaching of Jesus

Much of Jesus' teaching certainly insists on the identity between what God considers righteousness and the cause of the poor and outcast members of society—even when those outcast members are clearly identified as turned against God, as sinners. We have also seen a strain in some of the parables which showed unusual people like the Samaritan or the Gentile king of the Unforgiving Servant showing the compassion or forgiveness that is crucial to the realization of the love command. Many of the parables present human actions in a completely secular setting. Unlike their rabbinic counterparts, what is approved or disapproved is not presented as derived from specific precepts of the Law. The more secular setting implies that the ethical vision of the parables need not be limited to a Jewish context. This parable seems to confirm that impression. There is nothing grandiose or even very complex about its picture of judgment—nothing that requires detailed record keeping or attention to detailed precepts of the Law. Whether or not a person has aided "one of the least" will be as easy to determine as it is to teach a child to tell sheep and goats apart. Like the vineyard workers, there is no need in this picture of things for a detailed system of reward. The sheep are not sorted into separate classes according to the number of such people helped. Even motivation is not required. A person does not have to recognize Christ/God in the person. Perhaps the sheep acted as they did because they had listened to Moses and the prophets—unlike the Rich Man—or perhaps they acted simply out of compassion—like the Samaritan. In either case, the judgment is the same.

Human Significance

Though the parable is concerned with a particularly religious claim that humans are held responsible by God for their treatment of others, it does turn on issues that are still crucial ones for our society. The social structure makes it more difficult for an individual to aid some of the people mentioned directly than was the case in antiquity, yet there is not an issue on the list that is not a matter of pressing concern in some segment of our social life. Hunger, poverty, immigration, and prison conditions are staples of the nightly news and network public service programing. Sometimes that programing may tend to have the opposite effect to what is required. One becomes tired of the issue or feels that one has done one's part by sitting and listening to an hour documentary on prisons. Then the actual situations in which we as individuals might become involved with such issues through social, political or religious groups become insignificant or, worse, a "turn off." "I'm tired of hearing about starving people," one often hears people say. (Jas 2:14–17 suggests that the invisibility of the poor and hungry is not just a modern problem!) I know of one church group in North Dakota that became tired of hearing about the global problems of refugees. They knew that their small congregation could not do anything about that. Instead, they all got together and adopted a refugee family which is now a happy, popular and enriching part of all of their lives. Perhaps the experience of that group reminds us of the importance of Jesus' reduction in scale. Cosmic and global problems may make some issues seem so remote that we do not have to become involved in them. But there are smaller pieces to those bigger issues that can be tackled by local groups of people who want to accomplish something on their own. I never thought much myself about the food we contributed to the parish Thanksgiving collection until a priest from one of the parishes to which it was given happened to tell me how the food was stored and distributed to particularly destitute cases over the year, and of the efforts he was also making to educate the children in better eating habits—away from the heavy diet of junk food that is even more the lot of the poor than the middle class. Such small things might not seem worth much concern, yet the mixed metaphor of the parable in which the king is identified with the insignificant, suffering members of society suggests that for any society and any person such small things are as important as the great ones.

Religious Significance

We have seen that the dynamics of the story itself suggest a judgment which is applicable to humanity as a whole, which is clear-cut, and which does not require membership in a particular religious group. A person need not even recognize the real significance of the aid that he or she gives to such people. This perspective does not, of course, deny the claim that those instructed by the Law and the prophets or those seeking to be disciples of Jesus will have a special edge on others, since they recognize the overwhelming importance of such concerns. The listing of "works of mercy" in catechetical form reminds the audience of their own instruction.

A second exegetical question is raised by the expression "the least of these, my brethren." We have adopted the view that it applies to all of suffering humanity [as does Jeremias, who points to the "all the nations" in the introduction to the parable:207; also Meier:178]. Other exegetes point out that Matthew used the expression "little ones" throughout his gospel to refer to Christians, just as the expression "brethren" also frequently means simply fellow Christians. They argue that the passage means that non-Christians will be judged on the basis of how they treat suffering and persecuted Christians as in Mt 10:40–42; people are promised that those who aid the traveling missionaries will surely receive a reward.

Attempts to argue from the positioning of the parable in Matthew have also produced contrasting evaluations. The view that the passage refers to all humanity points out that this is the last section before the passion narrative. Jesus is about to "show" his identity with the poor and outcast in his death as an unrecognized and despised member of humanity [J. A. T. Robinson, 1962:91f]. Stendahl points to Jewish writings, called Testaments, which claimed to give the final instructions of the dying patriarch as the model for this section of Matthew. He argues that the section is not about how to get through the judgment but how to continue Jesus' absence. Christians are being instructed that any love or service that they would like to show to him, they should show to the least in the Christian community. Thus, he argues that the whole principle of love is directed toward other members of the community and is not concerned with outsiders at all [Stendahl:63]. This injunction would be parallel to the Matthean interpretation of the Lost Sheep, which instructed leaders to seek out the "least" in the community. Though this interpretation may well represent the Jewish Christian side of Matthew's theology, we still find the universal humanity reading more persuasive, since the pattern of the scene recalls Jewish models concerned with the judgment of the nations. That interpretation also seems to us to be better suited to the universalist and wisdom elements characteristic of Jesus' preaching.

Another theological issue that underlies this passage is the identification of Jesus with the suffering outcast. That identification implies that the Christian will not simply be involved with such problems on the basis of an humanitarian concern for the value of all persons. He or she is confronted with the claim that it is not possible to be indifferent to the plight of the suffering members of humanity and still claim a positive relationship with God. The parable does not imply that only religious people can address the needs and suffering of humanity. All people may be involved in doing so. But it does suggest that the Christian now has a special responsibility to address such issues. They are even more than issues of human rights and global justice; they are issues adopted by God himself as the crux of the relationship between the creator and his creatures.

Unjust Steward (Lk 16:1–8a)

The previous parable clearly made a claim on the audience for specific patterns of ethical behavior. This one seems to present the opposite. It is the type of parable that some suggest was designed to probe and test the limits of our neat moral universe. Crossan suggests that it depends upon the assumptions that are inherent in the parable of the Talents. Good servants are the ones who return a profit when the master reckons accounts [Crossan, 1973:108–110]. The applications which follow this parable show that it has been a problem for interpreters from the beginning. Verses 8b–9 draw an eschatological lesson: the steward is a shrewd child of this world, but the disciple will prove to be the shrewd child of the next. Verses 10–12 draw a moral lesson similar to that of the Talents: the disciple must be careful to manage well what has been entrusted to him or her. Verse 13 picks up a saying of Jesus (Mt 6:24; cp. GTh 47) on the dangers of wealth. The whole section is tied together by the theme of wealth and the danger that it poses for discipleship. We have already seen that Luke is very much concerned with such topics and frequently highlights lessons for wealthy Christians that may be derived from the parables.

Literary Analysis

The parable itself follows a clear structure. The central sections in direct discourse direct our attention to the actions of the servant.

I. ND, v. 1: introduction. The master learns about the servant. (Wasting goods may only mean that he is not returning the expected profit.)

II. DD, v. 2: master's verdict. This completes setting the scene, which leaves the parable to focus on what the steward will do.

III. DD, vv. 3–4: steward's evaluation of the situation and decision about a course of action. Each begins with the expression: "What shall I do?"

IV. DD, vv. 5–7: steward and the debtors. Two parallel episodes with men who owe one hundred measures of wheat/oil respectively.

V. ND, v. 8a: master's evaluation of the steward's action. He acted prudently or wisely. The adverb *phronimos* refers to practical action aimed at accomplishing some particular end. It does not have anything to do with virtue in the more general sense of justice.

Jeremias thinks that v. 8a refers to Jesus' commending the man's action as an example of how one might behave in a crisis. He suggests that it was aimed at those in the audience who were wavering and could not make up their mind about whether or not to follow him [46f]. However, we would argue that v. 8a represents the necessary ending to the story. Kyrios, Lord, still means the master in question. What is missing without it is any hint as to the direction the steward's action would really take. Is his idea a stupid one, given the situation? The commendation for prudent action gives us the necessary hint without spelling out any further details. The steward has reason to expect that this action will reach the goal that he is seeking.

A relatively clear actant diagram can be constructed for this story:

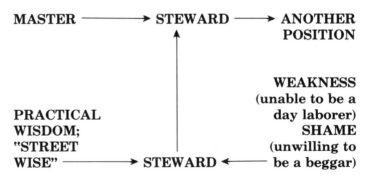

Note what the parable does not say. The shift to narrative at the end helps to emphasize the fact that the steward does not regain his standing with the master. It suggests that the master merely heard about what he had done and perhaps how he obtained another position. He gives him credit for a smart "bail out." Nor does the parable follow the pattern of Trickster tales in which the dumb master, letting the steward draw up the final accounts, is outsmarted by the clever fox [so Crossan, 1979:87]. There is no indication that the master is distressed by what the steward has done. Such evaluations are the result of the traditional way of titling the parable the "Unjust" Steward and of evaluating the man's conduct with reference to our standards rather than those of the first century.

Historical Background

We can see that there are enough hints in the structure of the story itself to send us looking for a different background than the one we might assume. We cannot accept Crossan's objection to the careful analysis of the background on the basis that laziness is the steward's vice and that the vice is what pushes him to find a solution [1974:110]. The steward would not have owned property, but his position as steward placed him well above that of the day laborers we met in the Talents. Deprived of his position, he would be reduced to their situation. In addition to social embarrassment, mentioned in regard to begging, the audience has no reason not to accept his own evaluation at face value. The man is in no physical condition to become a laborer. Remember that this man lives in a close knit society. What happens to him will be known to all—and apparently was, since the master knows at the end what he has done. Begging is a common feature of that society and would represent the depths of public embarrassment for such a person as the steward.

The situation of the debtors and the steward represents a fairly common picture of the time. People often had to borrow in order to meet taxes or gain seed for planting [Freyne: 182]. Since the Old Testament forbids taking interest, the interest due was figured into the amount borrowed and written down as such. In addition, the steward had a legitimate claim to add his own commission to the total bill. These arrangements suggest that the steward has not done anything outside the ordinary. One could only call it "unjust" insofar as the whole system represented a perversion of the intent of the prohibition against taking interest. The man has not deprived the master of anything that he would have gained had the steward stayed with the job. Perhaps the master expected to gain extra by collecting the steward's commission for himself, but the story does not give us any indication that such is the case.

The steward has "made friends" for himself by adjusting the accounts so as to remit his own share [Fitzmyer:175–177]. Whatever one says about the justice of the overall system, one is hard pressed not to give the steward credit for clever action in response to the problem. If the characterization of the steward as "unjust" in v. 8a is original, it is a reflection on the whole system of which he has taken advantage. It does not imply that he is a particularly wicked individual.

Teaching of Jesus

It is difficult to situate this parable in the context of Jesus' ministry. We have already seen that early Christians used it to comment on the dangers of wealth. The "unjust" of v. 8a may even derive from their use of the parable. They can see the whole system which created rich men and their stewards as "unjust," as creating additional burdens for the poorer farmers who were forced to borrow in order to plant or to meet tax assessments whenever the harvest had not been a good one. Jeremias suggested that this parable was directed at those who were wavering and that it was intended to point out the necessity for decisive action. The story itself indicates that the steward has made a realistic—if not too flattering—assessment of his situation and its likely outcome. Having made that assessment, he is able to use the only resources left to him to insure that he will be taken on by someone else, and the conclusion suggests that his plan was successful. If people who trade in such "unjust" profit are able to look at themselves in such a realistic fashion, then the waverers should also take a "long hard look" at themselves. This man had only one opportunity to get out of the situation. His "smarts" consist in his ability to recognize that opportunity and make use of it. Others would fail because they are not realistic enough about their situation or because they are unable to see the one opportunity for getting out of it. The attached sayings about wealth indicate that early Christians often found wealth to be an obstacle to a person's ability to size up his or her real standing with God. The Rich Man and Lazarus was a prime example of that situation. Perhaps this parable was an example of the kind of cleverness that some people can show and yet not see that they are faced with an equally crucial situation in their relationship with God. If so, it might serve to explain non-belief to disciples rather than to coax the waverers off the fence. However, the parable itself does not give us enough clues to make a specific application outside the suggestions provided by the sayings that early Christians attached to it. It should be clear that the parable is not approving the economic arrangements that the man has taken advantage of. It may even imply disapproval of the whole setup with its "unjust." These arrangements were a fact of life for the audience, however. They are being used to present an image of a certain kind of "smart" person—something the audience might admire, though not imitate, just as U.S. and British audiences admired the "smarts" by which J. R. Ewing in the TV series "Dallas" was always extracting himself from his shady business deals—at least until he was finally shot. The parable poses something of a question to the audience in another setting: How "smart" are you?

Human Significance

The popularity of J. R. Ewing in "Dallas" shows that people today have no difficulty in appreciating such shrewd characters—though one's relief at some of his escapes might be considerably lessened if the survival of the "good" members of his family were often not also at stake! Like the steward, J. R. acts out of a clear recognition of what kind of game he is playing; crises may set him back for a few minutes of deliberation, but they never put a permanent dent in his exterior style. Like the steward, he is not in total control of the fortune with which he is wheeling and dealing. In several episodes, he is almost put out altogether but always manages to get around the controls of his father and/or brother, both of whom he can often con into participating in his schemes. Part of his popularity rests on the ability he has to manipulate the system, which the whole script admits is fraught with such double-dealing. Most of his victims are not "innocent," since they are wealthy enough to be in the game too. The men with whom the steward is dealing are in a similar situation. They may be small farmers, and they may be in debt for wheat or oil, but they are not day laborers or beggars. Not only do they own land, but they also are in a position to have stewards of their own, since this steward hopes to be taken on by one of them.

Most people admire such cleverness "from below." We would not really want to be in J. R.'s situation, but we would like to have his ability to get out of the lesser scrapes and crises in which we find ourselves. Most people faced with unemployment break down for a while and are not able to think of anything to do—let alone come up with a plan for another job. This situation is particularly evident when a person is fired because he or she is not performing the job competently. Pleading and self-justification are the first responses, not realistic appraisal of oneself and one's situation. Poor students do the same thing. Those who appear to complain about a grade lower than what they think they deserve show an amazing ability to forget some bad test scores, missed classes, and late work. A quick check with a dean or another teacher will invariably show that the student has a pattern of such behavior. Rather than look at themselves and their abilities and plotting a better course for the future, such people invariably resort to whining, pleading or threats, hoping to be let out of the situation in which they find themselves. The solution would not emerge from a position of self-pity or an unrealistic view of what will happen to him afterward. Thus, the parable suggests that on the human level the really clever people have a virtue beyond their ability to wheel and deal. They know who and what they are. They do not live in a fantasy about themselves, their abilities, or the situations that they face. Such realism is an asset in many "crises" that everyone faces in his or her life. It enables one to come up with real solutions to those problems and hence represents the practical wisdom for which the steward is praised.

Religious Significance

We have seen that early Christians made various applications of the story to problems of wealth and discipleship. They also recognize that a certain shrewdness and practical wisdom is necessary for the disciples as well. Jesus' parables never suggest that religious people are to be naive about the complex actions and motivations of human beings. One has to begin with a clear recognition of one's own limitations and one's situation. At the same time, that recognition could be obscured by the concerns that dominate this man's life, so that although one appears to be prospering in a worldly sense, one is losing underneath it all. J. R.'s actions finally breed such a web of hatred that any one of several people could be responsible for his shooting. A person cannot really begin to follow Jesus' path of discipleship without such an acknowledgment of his or her individual character and situation. Many of the parables challenge us to see ourselves as we really are and not as we would like to appear either to ourselves or to others.

The Pharisee and the Publican (Tax-Collector) (Lk 18:9–14)

This brief parable presents another picture of how people estimate themselves. Verse 9 sets the parable in a context directed against those who think too much of their own righteousness. The prayer uttered by the Pharisee would not necessarily have been unusual as Jeremias' Jewish parallels show [142f]. The members of the Essene sect also thanked God that his grace made it possible for them to be among the righteous and not among the sinners of Israel. Such prayers were not necessarily manifestations of individual pride. The prayer often acknowledges the divine assistance which is required to live a life of fidelity to the Law. They are rejoicing in the life that God has made it possible for them to lead. Tax-collectors, on the other hand, were considered supreme examples of what it meant to be a sinner. They contracted to collect a certain sum and then made their own fortunes by collecting more than the sum they had agreed to turn over to the authorities. Some Jewish writings consider tax-collecting to be an occupation which leads a person to forfeit his status in the chosen people—as does the swineherding of the prodigal son. Thus, it is a term with strongly negative social overtones. According to such views, a person would have to give up his means of livelihood if he wished to reclaim his status as a pious Jew [Jeremias:143]. The tax-collector's prayer is a citation from Psalm 51:1, 19.

The parable may have been based on a Galilean proverb. The Pharisaic movement never gained the strong loyalty of the people in Galilee that it had in Judah to the south. Scott suggests that this parable could easily be converted to a proverb of the form: "Better to be a tax-collector who acknowledges his sin than a Pharisee who is self-righteous before God" [Scott, 1971:77]. The proverb is not so much a commendation of the tax-collector as a condemnation of the Pharisaic pattern of righteousness. At least the tax-collector knows that his occupation alienates him from God. Verse 14b attaches a proverb of eschatological reversal to the parable. It also appears in the context of woes against the Pharisees in Mt 23:12. There Christians are warned not to adopt the titles and hierarchical distinctions that are typical of such people. Luke has also retained the issue of self-exaltation and hierarchy in the sayings about how people seek places at a banquet.

Literary Analysis

The various sayings attached at the beginning and the end do not belong to the parable. The reader is left to his or her own evaluation of the situation.

I. V. 10: ND, Introduction
II. Vv. 11–12: The Pharisee, ND: his posture
               DD: his prayer
III. V. 13: The Tax-collector, ND: his posture
               DD: his prayer
IV. V. 14a: DD, Narrator's comment

The key to the dynamics of this parable can be found in the inverse parallelism implied in the two descriptions:

	Pharisee	*Tax-collector*
Posture:	standing before him	standing at a distance
		would not lift up his eyes to heaven
		but beat his breast
	prayed thus:	saying:
prayer:	God,	God,
	I give you thanks, that I am not like the rest of men,	have mercy on me,
	thieves,	a sinner.

> unjust,
> adulterers,
> or like this tax-
> collector.
> I fast twice a
> week, and pay
> tithes on all that
> I own.

The two prayers form a striking contrast in length. The tax-collector has little to say, while the Pharisee catalogues the piety for which he is giving God thanks. On the other hand, the tax-collector's posture is all important. It describes more than any words could the distance that he feels between himself and God. One could even say that it represents his assent to the sentiments expressed by the Pharisee when he concludes his list of possible sinners with a glance back toward the tax-collector. The tax-collector acknowledges his distance from the kind of righteousness represented by the Pharisee and yet hopes that God will still hear his request for mercy. The parable's conclusion leaves it up to the audience to decide which of these two is really made righteous by his prayer.

Teaching of Jesus

The parable may have been another that was provoked by the charges that Jesus was "friend of tax-collectors and sinners" (e.g., Lk 15:1f). Such a charge is as much a way of slandering someone as it is an indication of the groups with whom Jesus spent his time. It is voiced by enemies who wish to discredit Jesus in the eyes of the people. This parable is similar to sayings in Mt 9:13 where Jesus' eating with such people is criticized after he has called one of them as a disciple. The answer implied in this parable is that it is possible for a tax-collector to find favor with God through an honest acknowledgement of his sinfulness and prayer for mercy. If the parable is based on a common proverb, then it would be using a piece of popular wisdom about "the righteous Pharisees" to discredit those who were trying to attack Jesus' association with such people by saying that even you would rather be a tax-collector than a Pharisee!

Human Significance

The story is a good example of what social psychologists have in mind when they speak of people internalizing a negative identity. The two men assume positions and postures that are ascribed to them by the social definition of their relative worth. The Pharisee expresses everything that his society recognizes as reprehensible, and then sees that summed up before his very eyes in the tax-collector. The tax-collector's hesitant entry into the temple, his position at the back, and his posture when praying all express the same evaluation of himself that is put forward by the society at large. He barely has a right to be there in the temple. He hopes that God will still hear his prayer despite his status as "sinner."

There are many examples of people who take on such negative self-images. Some delinquents are simply "acting out" the role of "bad child" that has always been ascribed to them. Minority groups will sometimes insist on their own inferiority, an implicit acknowledgement of the judgments passed by others in the society. Real equality requires an internal as well as an external transformation so that the persons belonging to the group in question "feel" themselves to be as good, as smart, as competent or whatever as other members of the society. Of course, the Pharisee's prayer raises another difficult issue. Religious symbols can be used to foster such inequality even when they were certainly not intended to create such divisions. Does a person who is going to make the sacrifices that the Pharisee does require someone who is clearly "unrighteous," clearly a sinner? In other words, does the presence of certain socially despised persons reinforce the values and ethical commitments of the rest of a society? There are many examples in which the despised, the good-for-nothings, etc., do play such a role. I can remember being admonished as a child in the south, by my mother and other southern relatives and by blacks who sometimes looked after us, not to do certain things because "white trash does that," or having certain shacks and people pointed out to me with the expression "Them's white trash." There was no question in any of our minds that one had to hold to certain social norms in order to escape the fate of being "white trash." In the affluent Boston suburb where I grew up such groups were less readily available, though some things were attributed to one or another ethnic group. The general norm was the all pervasive "One does/does not do 'x'." Exactly what I would become if I failed to toe that norm was never so clear as it was with the threat of being "white trash." During the 1960's the "hippies" and the "Hare Krishnas" on the Boston streets took on that role for my youngest brother. At age four and five, he would walk resolutely across the Public Garden refusing to see any such persons. They were the epitome of everything bad and should be avoided at all costs. The tax-collector plays that role for the Pharisee. The other sins that he mentions are not "public" in the way in which the tax-collector is publicly evil. Doubtless the Pharisee would also instruct his son to keep the Law faithfully and to avoid being the tax-collector type of Jew. The problems created by violating such boundaries are not peculiar to Jesus' behavior. They are still part of our own efforts at social integration and equality. How can a person feel anything but anger and revulsion at being required to associate with those who symbolize what his or her culture has taught him or her to despise? How can a person not feel that the very ethical fabric of his or her society is threatened when such demands are made? The issue goes beyond whether or not the tax-collector is a nice individual or a person you really would like to have as a neighbor, since association with that person seems to symbolize accepting all the negative things associated with that person. For the Pharisee, it would have felt like becoming a sinner.

Religious Significance

Jesus' claims about tax-collectors and sinners appear as more threatening than they perhaps seemed at first when translated into terms of such social dynamics. The parable might be said to ameliorate the situation in two ways. It appeals to a popular saying among the audience which does permit a higher valuation on a tax-collector than on a Pharisee, and it presents his sinfulness and prayers for mercy. He is not the arrogant, hardhearted sinner who knows nothing about God that some might think him to be. Thus the audience may be able to show him some sympathy. The poor man hardly dares to come in the temple; he certainly will not try to look up to heaven. Such a person might be accepted, since he is not flaunting the values of the audience but serving as an example of piety.

Luke places this parable after that of the Unjust Judge as a comment upon prayer. Mt 6:5, 7 contrasts brevity and lack of ostentation at prayer with the prayer of the Pharisees. It is possible that the parable was already used among Jewish Christians to distinguish their prayer from that of their Jewish neighbors.

Summary

The variety of characters in these parables is striking. The pious or the officially righteous are not the only ones who appear as examples for the instruction of Jesus' audience. We find that anyone can be held responsible for the conduct toward the suffering members of humanity. The judgment is no more difficult to make than sorting a flock. Even the less esteemed members of society, shrewd stewards and tax-collectors, may serve as examples and warnings for the disciple. All of the parables show that the ethical stance recommended by Jesus is firmly rooted in society. The disciple is not expected to be separated from or naive about the world in which most people live and the motives that lead them to act in different ways. They are to be realistic both about themselves and others. This realism makes it impossible for a person to use the excuse that the world is "too evil or too corrupt" a place for the kind of obedience that Jesus expects. Such realism should also protect the Christian from the barriers of self-righteousness or the type of religious dynamics that requires symbolization of the things one seeks to avoid in a particular group of people. One is not permitted the luxury of self-congratulations—"Thank God I'm not like that"—if "that" can in fact be an example of piety, and perhaps even one of the sheep in the final reckoning. Once again, breaking down the barriers between people requires our suspension of judgment, not a lack of ethical standards.

STUDY QUESTIONS

1. How do the parables go about teaching ethical behavior?

2. Why is the "scale" of the parables an important factor in Jesus' ethical teaching?

3. What does the Sheep and the Goats suggest about the judgment? What is the relationship between its norm for judgment and God?

4. Why is the Sheep and the Goats located at the end of the discourses of Jesus in Matthew?

5. What would you have done in the Unjust Steward's situation? Would you have hired him if you were one of the debtors?

6. Try to think of other examples of the Pharisee-publican relationship. How do people today react to such comments as the Pharisee makes?

Chapter Eleven

GOD AND HIS PEOPLE

The universalism implied in the parables raises some questions which Christians today often find difficult to appreciate. Remember Jesus was speaking to a Jewish audience. He and they had been brought up to believe that they were the chosen people of God. They had a relationship to him which was not the same as that of any of the other peoples on earth, since they had the revelation in the Law. Though the Gentile nations might be converted to Judaism, the people of Israel would have pride of place in the messianic age. All would stream to her capital and her God. We have seen that the Mustard Seed posed a severe challenge to such grandiose expectations. It suggested that one could be "people of God" without the great national exaltation that some people expected. Now other parables suggest that anyone may show the compassion required for salvation—a possibility not unknown to Jesus' Jewish contemporaries. Yet the questions of national salvation and sinfulness could hardly be avoided as Jews saw themselves among the least nations of the earth, dominated by yet another great empire.

Renewing the People of God

Sometimes Christians picture the ministry of Jesus as aimed at converting individuals. The reduction of many of the great images to the level of individual experience would certainly support such a conclusion. But Jeremias and others warn us against falling into the trap of supposing that the individuals in the parables represent an individualistic focus to Jesus' mission. They insist that the language of rule of God also associated with Jesus' preaching refers primarily to the issue of the experience of a people as "chosen," the people ruled by God. We have also seen that the metaphors of God as loving father apply not to individuals but to the people as God's chosen, adopted "son." Ancient religion in general has much less interest in private religious experience than in its public, social and traditional manifestations. Jesus may be reducing certain images to the scale of individual life as part of a larger attempt to renew the religious tradition of his people. We have seen that he challenged many of their assumptions.

Some of the assumptions about national greatness and judgment that appear to be rejected in the parables may have been behind the perplexity that people felt over their status as God's people. Their image of the world—a world in which most people are evil and will be condemned, while the righteous can only barely hang on to be saved, but if they do, they can be exalted and exult in their salvation over those who have tormented them—never appears in Jesus' parables. The world is not so dangerous that the righteous have to avoid all association with sinners. In fact, one cannot necessarily tell who would qualify as righteous and who as condemned in the world in which we find ourselves. Jesus will never accept a vision of holiness that requires separation from others or from the world or that permits one person to be exalted over another. The disciples will later find the universality of Jesus' vision expanded as they actually include the Gentiles in their communities.

A second part of Jesus' picture concerns the "visibility" of God's action. Some people expected his concern to be apparent on the large scale of national events. Jesus' God stands behind the poor, the outcast, and the prisoner, but he does not emerge into direct view. Even the righteous may not have recognized the close association between their aid to such people and the God who stands behind them. God also stands behind many of the parables. He is not one of the characters but the support for a given type of relationship between people as opposed to a different one. There are no clear signs that distinguish those who are righteous from those who are not in this world. That has to be determined by God in the judgment, even though the criteria on which he will do so are not complex. God's hiddenness on the large scale seems to be the presupposition of his presence to his people in the least details of what appear to be the most insignificant lives.

From the perspective of many in Jesus' audience, his rejection of some of the righteous people may have seemed puzzling. He suggests that they must become reconciled with some of those who symbolize everything that their piety has warned them against. The stories of the prophets and the example of John the Baptist were evidence enough that prophets do not always have an easy time in Israel. But people expected a messianic renewal that would be different. Righteousness would spring up throughout the people or be created by the appearance of the messiah as judge to destroy evil when it had gained too great a hold. Jesus does not seem to fit in either category. Many of the righteous are dubious about his ministry. After his death and resurrection, when the disciples no longer had any doubts about whether Jesus really was God's chosen messiah or not, they still found that most Jews were not sure. Instead, large numbers of Gentiles responded to their preaching. Thus, the conversion of the Gentiles does not derive from the renewal of the whole people of Israel as a shining example but only from the efforts of a small sect of Jewish Christians. That is something that most Christians take for granted, but which must have been a considerable surprise to the first Christians. What has God intended now? Some concluded that the failure of the Jewish revolt against Rome and the destruction of the temple in A.D. 70 was proof that God had finally given up on his old people and had decided to create a new people from among the Gentiles. We have already seen that Jesus is careful not to leave room for such conclusions. He allows the possibility that the truly righteous will be taken care of by God even if they do not respond to his preaching. Yet God is presented as seeking to be God of all, not of a limited number of the righteous. Rejection of Jesus cannot be allowed to frustrate that plan.

Wicked Tenants (Mk 12:1–11//Mt 21:33–44//Lk 20:9–18; GTh 65)

This parable has been elaborately allegorized so as to refer to the destruction of Jerusalem and suggest that God has chosen himself new people. These new tenants must be faithful where the old ones were not. The killing of the heir is an allegory for the crucifixion of Jesus as Matthew/Luke make clear. GTh 65 preserves a version which is a rather simple outline of the plot of the opening part of the parable:

> There was a man who owned a vineyard. He leased it to tenants so that they might work it, and he might collect the produce from them. He sent his servant for the tenants to give him the produce of the vineyard. They seized his servant and beat him, almost killing him. The servant returned and told his master. The master said, "Perhaps they did not recognize him." He sent another servant. The tenants beat this one as well. Then the owner sent his son, saying, "Perhaps they will respect my son." But the tenants knew it was the heir to the vineyard; they seized him and killed him.

The simpler structure of the GTh version will help us sort out the allegorical additions that have been made in the other versions. The original probably had two single servant missions followed by that of the son such as we find here. Additional servants have been added in the others, since all the evangelists see the parable as an allegory of salvation history. The servant wounded in the head in Mark probably refers to John the Baptist. Matthew/Luke have the murder of the son outside the vineyard, which brings it into line with the crucifixion.

Some argue that the reference to Is 5:2 in Matthew/Mark was an early Christian addition, since the vineyard stands for Israel [Crossan, 1973:91–95; Jeremias:70]. Others argue that it is the basis for the whole parable [Dodd:97ff; Carlston:185, who thinks the whole parable is an early Christian allegory]. The allusion fits the indirect style of Jesus' use of the Old Testament. The evangelists have explicit citations following the parable. Though the activities are also characteristic of preparing a vineyard to rent, the audience would certainly recognize the images

Fig. 11: PARALLEL VERSIONS OF
THE WICKED TENANTS

MATTHEW	MARK	LUKE
There was a householder	A man	A man
who planted a vineyard	planted a vineyard	planted a vineyard
and set a hedge around it	and set a hedge around it	
and dug a wine press in it	and dug a pit for the wine press	
and built a tower	and built a tower	
and let it out to tenants	and let it out to tenants	and let it out to tenants
and went into another country.	and went into another country.	and went into another country.
When the season of fruit drew near,	When the time came,	When the time came,
he sent his servants to the tenants to get	he sent a servant to the tenants to get from them	he sent a servant to the tenants that they should give him
his fruit,	some of the fruit of the vineyard.	some of the fruit of the vineyard;
and the tenants took his servants	And they took him	but the tenants
and beat one,	and beat him,	beat him,
killed another,		
and stoned another.	and sent him away empty-handed.	and sent him away empty-handed.
Again he sent other servants	Again he sent to them another servant,	And he sent another servant,
more than the first,		

	and they wounded him in the	him also they beat
and	head, and	and
they did the same to them.	treated him shamefully.	treated shamefully, and sent him away empty-handed.
	And he sent another and him they killed; and so with many others. Some they beat, and some they killed.	And he sent yet a third; this one they wounded and cast out.
Afterward he sent his son to them, saying,	He had still one other, a beloved son; finally he sent him to them, saying,	The owner of the vineyard said, "What shall I do? I will send my beloved son.
"They will respect my son."	"They will respect my son."	Perhaps they will respect him."
But when the tenants	But those tenants	But when the tenants
saw the son,		saw him,
they said to themselves,	said to one another,	they said to themselves,
"This is the heir;	"This is the heir;	"This is the heir;
come, let us kill him, and	come, let us kill him and	let us kill him that
have his inheritance."	the inheritance will be ours."	the inheritance may be ours."
And they took him	And they took him	
and cast him out of the vineyard,		And they cast him out of the vineyard,
and killed him.	and killed him,	and killed him.
	and cast him out of the vineyard.	

When, therefore, the owner of the vineyard comes,		
what will he do to those tenants?	What will the owner of the vineyard do?	What then will the owner of the vineyard do?
They said to him,		
	He will come and	He will come and
"He will put those wretches		
to a miserable death, and let out the vineyard to other tenants, who will give him the fruits in their seasons."	destroy the tenants, and give the vineyard to others.	destroy the tenants, and give the vineyard to others.

of God's love and care for his people from their tradition. Jesus has somewhat shifted the metaphor. The prophetic song dealt with the relationship between a man and his unproductive vineyard. This parable focuses on a metaphor more common to Jesus' audience—the owner and his tenants.

With the Isaiah allusion the ending of the parable with a question would be more than enough to lead the hearer to the conclusion that the owner will act in anger. Verse 9 makes the expectations of the audience more explicit. Matthew has typically added a condition for the new tenants: they will fulfill the conditions of the contract. Some interpreters insist that the simpler version of the parable that has been elaborated by each evangelist may have contained the Isaiah allusion but was an early Christian allegory, not a parable of Jesus. It was to account for the Gentile mission by showing that God had intended it from the beginning or for God's turning from the Jews to the Christians, since Jesus had been condemned to death by the Jews [see Carlston:187–190]. Arguments against such interpretations require us to indicate a non-allegorical treatment of other issues relevant to Jesus' ministry behind this story [e.g. Jeremias:75; Dodd:96, 102]. Dodd cannot interpret the parable without seeing it as a judgment by Jesus on his own generation and an implied recognition of the hostility that would lead to his death. Jeremias, on the other hand, once again suggests that it is a vindication of Jesus' mission to outcasts and sinners: he is going to prove the faithful tenant where the pious of his generation have failed.

Literary Analysis

The structure of the story emphasizes the pattern of violence by the tenants which culminates in the death of the son. Unlike the Unjust Steward in which the steward had to respond to decisive action by the master, this story focuses on a series of incidents in which such decisive action is strangely lacking or ill-advised. One might even think that the owner's actions have simply brought on greater violence.

    I. ND, v. 1: introduction, leased vineyard.
    II. ND, vv. 2–5: wrongdoing of the tenants, oriented around words sending and receiving.
    III. DD, v. 6: Owner's decision; sends his son.
    IV. DD, v. 7: Tenant's deliberation: Let's get the vineyard.
    V. ND, v. 8: Tenants' action: Kill the son.
    VI. DD, v. 9a: Narrator's question: What's to happen next?

The beating of the first two servants heightens the suspense, since the audience is unsure what the owner will do in response. Crossan reminds us that we should focus on the brutal murder of the son. Sometimes the common allegory of the parable in which the son=Jesus deprives us of the shock associated with that feature of the story, since Christians have come to see the death of Jesus as more than a brutal murder.

Read without allegorical adjustments, the story raises some difficult questions. Certainly the death of the son is a tragedy for the owner. Was he foolish to send his son to collect from such tenants? Why does he persist in trying to collect his rent according to the usual means? Why doesn't he use force equal to that of the tenants to throw them out? Is there any chance that even our instinctual reaction to the end of the story—he'll come, punish the tenants and get others—is wrong? Might he still try to collect the rent?

Historical Background

We have a difficult time knowing how to respond to such questions without some sense of the legal arrangements that underlie this story. We have some evidence from Egyptian papyri of the period that illuminate the contractual arrangements between the owner and his tenants and something of the violence that could also break out in attempts by some people to gain the property of others. The owner might well be responsible for certain preparations prior to leasing his land. The contract would also stipulate that at the appropriate time he or his agents could collect the stated rent. Here is such a contract. You can see that the introduction of the parable invokes just such an arrangement:

Contract for Labor in a Vineyard
and Lease of a Fruit Garden

(An introduction named the parties to the contract and their villages.) We voluntarily undertake to lease for one year more from Hathur 1 of the present 6th year all the vine-tending operations in the vineyard owned by you in the area of the village of Tanais and the adjoining reed plantation . . . which operations are, concerning the vineyard, plucking of reeds, collection and transport of them, proper pruning, making them into bundles, binding, stripping and transport of leaves and throwing them outside the mud walls, layering as many vine shoots as necessary, digging, scooping hollows around the vines and trenching. You, the landlord, being responsible for the arrangement of the reeds, and we for assisting you in the work; we being responsible for the remaining operations; namely, breaking up the ground, picking off shoots, keeping the vines well-tended, giving space to the growths, cutting back and thinning foliage as needed; . . . further we agree to assist you in the vineyard and in the reed plantation in superintending the asses which bring the earth in order that it will be thrown in the proper places. And we will test the jars for the wine and put them, when they have been filled, in the open-air shed, and plaster them, and move the wine, and strain it from one jar into another, and watch over them as long as they are stored in the shed. The wage for all the above operations being 4500 silver drachmae, 10 artabae of wheat and 4 jars of wine at the vat, which we are to receive in installments according to the progress of the operations. Likewise we undertake to lease for one year the produce of all the date palms and fruit trees in the old vineyard, of which we will pay as special rent: $1\frac{1}{2}$ artabae of walnut dates; $1\frac{1}{2}$ of fresh dates; $1\frac{1}{2}$ of pressed dates; $\frac{1}{2}$ of black olives; 500 selected peaches; 15 citrons; 400 summer figs before the inundation; 500 winter figs; and 4 large, fat melons.

Moreover we will in consideration of the above wages plough the adjoining fruit garden to the south of the vineyard, and do the watering, weeding, and all the other seasonal operations; only the arrangement of reeds and the strewing of earth being left to you the landlord; *the rent being secured against all risks.* If our undertaking is guaranteed to us, we will perform all the seasonal operations of the vineyard, the fruit garden, and the reed-plantation, at the *proper times* and to your satisfaction, *your agents keeping a check on everything and we will pay the special rent at the required time without delay;* and at the end of the period we will deliver the objects of the lease under cultivation well cared for and free from rushes, weeds and all coarse grass; *you having the right of execution upon us who are mutual securities for the payment of rent* as is fitting.

This undertaking is valid; and in answer to the formal question we have given our consent. (date, names and signatures of the parties)

This lengthy contract indicates that everything in the story is according to accepted legal custom. The owner sends an agent to collect his rent at the proper time. But the tenants in the parable are hardly model tenants. This contract indicates that the rent is to be paid no matter what the actual harvest is, and that the tenants are to pay without delay. The tenants in the parable certainly fail to meet those conditions. Instead they beat up the agent.

What evidence can we find that might explain such an outburst of violence? Josephus reports that some pro-Herodian nobles were drowned in the Sea of Galilee by the populace [Ant 415ff; 432ff]. They may have been some of those settled on rich farmland by Herod after he came to power in the area. In addition, there are many examples from legal papyri in Egypt of disputes over land that has been seized through violence and of intimidation that has been used against people to force them off their land. Usually, the violence does not come from below—tenants as here—but from someone richer and more powerful than the person who has the right to the land. Someone who owned land in another village might be particularly vulnerable, since local sentiment would keep people from aiding the tenants in protecting an outsider's property. Here is the testimony from a lawsuit filed by a man who had lost property in that way. He eventually had the land returned to him, and those who had seized it landed in jail:

Violent Seizure of Property in the Owner's Absence

There is an estate not far from the Zeus temple. . . . My kinsman bought this estate for me while I was away in Egypt; but certain men from Mysia took it wrongfully, first uttering every kind of threat and then resorting to actions. Being really desperate . . . they got together as many servants as they could, and laborers, and came on with weapons of all sorts. Some of them threw their spears and slung bullets of clods and stones from a distance, while others closed hand-to-hand; some advanced on the house and treated whatever was in it as their own. All was chaos and bloodshed. When report was made of these events at Pergammum, I was hardly able to breathe; but there was a trial. I was at a loss to know what to do.

This man's suit makes it clear that violence and beatings are not out of the question in village life.

These people did not succeed in keeping control of the land. What about violence against the actual heir such as we find in the parable told by Jesus. Here is an example, though it stops short of actual murder. Those who are most vulnerable are the widowed, the handicapped, or the young. Here is an example of a plea from a case that has been in the court for two years, and the plaintiff has no relief in sight:

Violence Against Helpless Heirs

To the prefect of Egypt, from Gemellus of Antinoe, land-holder at Karanis. Some time ago, my lord, our father died leaving me and my sisters as heirs, and we took over his possessions without opposition from anyone. Likewise, when my uncle died, I entered into his prop-erty without hindrance. But now Julius and Sotas wrongfully, with violence and arrogance, entered my fields after I had sown them and carried away a substan-tial amount of hay; not only that but he also cut dried olive shoots and heath plants from my olive grove. When I came there at the time of the harvest, I learned that he had committed these transgressions. In addition, not content, he again trespassed with his wife and a cer-tain Zenas, intending to hem in my cultivator with mal-ice so that he should abandon his labor . . .

(Two years later Gemellus is still filing petitions with the prefect:) I appeal, my lord, against Kastor, the tax-collector's assistant of the village of Karanis. This person who held me in contempt because of my infirmi-ty—for I have only one eye and I do not see with it though it appears to have sight, so that I am utterly helpless in both—first publicly abused me and my moth-er, after maltreating her with numerous blows and de-molishing all four doors of mine with an ax so that our house is wide open and accessible to every malefactor—though we owed no taxes, and for this reason he dared not even produce a receipt, lest he be convicted through it of injustice and extortion.

This man may not live near the field at Karanis, though the sec-ond suit suggests that at least some of the time he is there with his mother. Several individuals from the village are named as de-fendants. The first plea concerns violence against the man's property, the second against attempts by a tax-collector to extort money. One suspects that the first plea was not successful, since the violence against Gemellus continues. Clearly, those who are absent or perceived as too young to defend themselves are the victims of such violence.

The tenants in Jesus' parable are more extreme than any of the examples. Possibly they presume that the father has died and know that without the son there are no other heirs. The examples of redress through local courts and appeal to the prefect also suggest that the father may not be able to march into the village and take matters into his own hand—though such vengeance would not be considered out of order for the time. This parable is a conceivable extension of the kind of violence represented in these texts. The audience may well be horrified at such violence—just as we are when riots break out in our cities—but the situation of violence exists that could spawn such an incident. That is really all that is needed. These examples also make the actant diagram for this story clear:

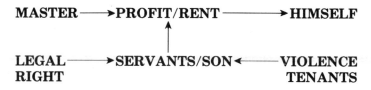

It turns out that the legal rights of the master are not sufficient to prevent the violence of the tenants. The owner may have some chance of getting the authorities to intervene in his behalf, but that is not an automatic process. He could find the legal system as unresponsive as the second man did. Meanwhile the tenants have the vineyard. Thus, the parable is firmly rooted in the realities of what could happen at the time of Jesus. The allusion to Is 5 indicates that he has more in mind than generalizing from contemporary experience of violence—or perhaps from a particular terrible incident known to the audience. The story is to point out a lesson about the people of God. The legal examples available suggest that the audience may hope that the owner will now take blood vengeance for his son, but that legal remedies may take much more time than has already elapsed. They also indicate a possible reason for his attempts to deal with the tenants according to the contract even after they have beaten the first servant. Should he have taken legal action sooner? Did the tenants presume that once they had beaten up the first servant they would have nothing to lose, since they certainly would not be able to renew their lease once the present one had expired? The owner is clearly in something of a bind. Contrary to the allegory which has him send several servants at once—certainly enough to manage the kind of violence that is represented in such incidents—he does not have a great number of servants or supporters to muster and take matters into his own hands. Like the lease cases above, he is presented as a person who leases land that he owns in a nearby village, not as a wealthy landowner. Like the landlord in the lease, he does some of the work himself. Both he and his son are known to the tenants who may have even assisted in preparing the vineyard. Notice that the version preserved in GTh makes recognition a key in the master's decision to send another servant. The tenants should certainly resist unauthorized attempts to grab some of the produce such as that demonstrated by the "assistant" tax-collector in Gemellus' suit. These indications of the realities of life under such a system make it clear that the concluding question is not an idle one. What should the master do? Certainly, he will eventually have to see that the tenants are punished, but is the personal vengeance suggested by the conclusion to the story in Matthew the only or even a likely answer?

Teaching of Jesus

The Isaiah reference suggests that this tale is meant to tell us something about God's relationship with his people. We have already seen that Jesus does not share the widespread expectation that God will have to step in soon and take horrible vengeance on all the evil people of the world who are tormenting the righteous and disregarding his Law. Is God in the same kind of bind as the owner of the vineyard? No one is in doubt about what the tenants' behavior deserves, but the problem is how the owner can realize the claim that he has on the tenants.

The owner in the story continues to pursue the contractual arrangements that he had with the tenants to the bitter end. Even after they have beaten two of his servants, he hopes that he can invoke the authority of the legal bond between them by sending a representative whom they should all recognize is not an impostor—his son. But it is up to the tenants themselves to break off the cycle of violence in which they have been engaged. Such an image certainly fits Jesus' presentation of God and his own ministry. It could be said to be a very practical representation of how to "overcome evil with good." One does not invoke legal sanctions or personal power against the first or even the second insult; rather, one continues to appeal to the relationship as it should be. Certainly the parable addresses a fundamental issue in Jesus' ministry—though not simply a vindication of his preaching to the poor as Jeremias claimed. The question is what disobedience and rejection mean in terms of God's relationship with his people. Jesus does not deny that the people are hardly sterling examples of piety—he has the prophetic image before the audience if they need any reminder! But he presents an image which suggests that God will continue to appeal. He will go to any lengths—even beyond those imagined by his audience—to reach the original goal without violent intervention.

Human Significance

This parable is a striking image of escalating violence in a situation in which the social and legal structures were clearly too weak to deal with what could and did occur among people. The owner is not the object of such violence because he is unusually cruel. His arrangements are on the small scale, between people who would at least know each other even if they did not belong to the same village. He is not a powerful person like those of Herod's supporters who were drowned in the Sea of Galilee. But that too is a matter of our own experience with such outbreaks of violence. The people who suffer its consequences are very often not the ones who are responsible for the socio-economic causes of the violence. The people who suffer from it are those who are close at hand and weak enough to appear vulnerable, people who will not be able to get speedy redress through the courts or from the local governor. Perhaps the best they can do is to carry on the hope that the violence will stop somewhere, preferably before they have suffered some irreparable loss such as this man has.

But the parable does not hold out any pollyanna solution to such problems. Here is a person who holds on as best he can and loses his only son in the bargain. The audience cannot help but wonder if he should have taken matters in hand sooner and exercised force against the tenants. After all, once they have broken their relationship with him, they have nothing more to lose. The punishment for beating one servant will not be considerably less than for beating two. They even come to see murder as a possible solution to the whole situation! Certainly the story can serve as a warning about the way in which violence can breed in situations of weak legal and social custom. It is likely that the tenants even have the "sympathy" or at least the compliance of their fellow villagers. What will the owner do? Many a city and state official has found him or herself asking just that question after the situation has already exploded. One thing is certainly clear: never ignore the warning signals. If one is going to act like the owner—who may not have had any other alternative except coming himself—then one may have to reckon with some unpleasant consequences.

Religious Significance

The parable suggests not only that God himself identifies with the poor and weak outcasts of society but that he deals with his people as the weaker members of society must do. They have no choice; for God, one presumes, it is a policy of his own. Humans may use violence and vengeance to deal with situations of injustice; God will not. He will even go to limits that we would insist are intolerable. God does not come to work vengeance against humanity; he continues to appeal for what is due him. This appeal must be predicated on the assumption that escalating violence and rebellion is not the only response humans can/will make. They can also turn around at any time and show themselves to be "good tenants." From this perspective, the evangelists' allegorizing of the parable as one of salvation-history—servant after servant—simply brings out part of the dynamics of the story. Where they miss the mark, perhaps, is in the conclusion. God will finally come to destroy those tenants and give his vineyard to new ones. Since they knew themselves to be "faithful people" who had responded to God's call and since the Jews had recently suffered a disastrous defeat, the conclusion was not difficult to reach. However, it does not quite fit with the image of God's action that seems to underlie this parable. We all may know from the first what the tenants deserve if the case were being decided by a swift and impartial court of law, but such execution is not the point. The tenants must turn around, stop their own illegal violence, and give the owner what he is owed.

We have suggested that this parable is also a good image of what is implied in Jesus' policy of non-violence and love of enemy. Retaliation, legal or otherwise, is out. One must simply continue to pursue the relationship that should exist between oneself and the other party, hoping that the other party will then step into the role defined by that relationship. But, once again, Jesus is not naive about human behavior. The ability to pursue such relationships will also require the ability to take repeated "beatings" or worse. This dimension of the story makes it clear that Dodd is correct in associating it with the death of Jesus. Jesus did not necessarily speak directly about himself as the son as the later allegory had him do. But he did speak directly about his policy of non-retaliation and its possible consequences. Such a picture of the human situation makes it clear that Jesus could hardly have been too surprised at the violence that led to his death. Certainly that is not the way in which he or God would have liked Israel to respond, but it is a possible outcome of a deliberate policy of dealing with evil by pursuing what is just and good and not by massive punishment and cosmic vengeance. God continually appeals to the people to stand in the proper relationship with him, but he will never compel them to do so. In short, he does not act the way most of us would if subjected to such outrageous abuse!

Unjust Judge (Lk 18:1–8); Help at Midnight (Lk 11:5–8)

God's policy may be fine in the long run, but from the point of view of the righteous and oppressed among his people it may appear that God is not concerned about their plight. Luke preserves two short parables in the context of teaching about prayer that may have been addressed to this issue. They are based on the logic that if a person can prevail in awkward human situations, "how much the more" can one be confident that God responds to the prayers of the righteous people who are suffering for his cause. Both parables are probably derived from the wisdom tradition. The importunate neighbor has something of the sarcastic note with which the wisdom tradition looks at the varieties of human friendship. Friendship itself may not get us up, but persistent inconvenience will. The parable of the Unjust Judge is typical of the poor trapped in the complexities of the legal system. It may be an illustration of Prov 25:15:

> With patient persistence a high official may be persuaded, and a soft tongue can break stone.

The audience knows that God is not an unjust judge nor the importuned friend. He will not require such lengths of persistence before responding to the needs of his people. These parables do not claim that God responds immediately to individual petitions, nor do they suggest that God will suddenly shift the way in which he deals with his people. But they assure the righteous that God does hear, that their suffering does not pass for nothing, and that God's "invisible" action and persistent appeal to his people to repent does not imply that his justice is weak. Violence and injustice are still the objects of divine judgment.

Summary

These parables indicate that Jesus' vision of God and his action was addressed to the pressing issues of God's relationship with his people—both those who seem to have turned away from him and those who suffer the consequences of others' injustice. God cannot be read as a human writ large. He may appear to tolerate evil and injustice in a way that we could never imagine. Yet that tolerance is part of the remarkable love and concern that God has for all his creation. Such a stance—and Jesus' willingness to incarnate it in his own ministry—requires an extraordinary trust in humanity. Yet it is clearly a trust that knows full well the worst that humans are capable of doing as well as their best. God refuses to break off his covenant with the people no matter what they may do in response. He refuses to use the methods of vengeance and retaliation that we humans would certainly resort to in such cases of injustice. Thus one can see an image of God as one who will go to the absolute limit in treating his people as "in his favor," as capable of a renewed relationship with him. They must repent and turn back to the relationship with God that the covenant requires; they cannot/will not be forced to do so. God does not countenance the barriers of hostility and violence that people set up between one another. According to Jesus' vision, he does not even tolerate them in the context of religious perfection or defense of his own righteousness by excluding the sinner. God is willing apparently to go on appealing: the prophets, John the Baptist, Jesus, and Jesus' disciples after him are charged with the kind of out-going mission which represents God's cause in the world. God's message for the poor and outcast and his demand for justice will not be forced violently on his creation. It can only be represented and realized through the efforts of those who are willing to take up the obligation of preaching it to the nations.

STUDY QUESTIONS

1. Give two reasons why the relationship between God and his people was a matter of religious concern in the first century A.D.

2. How does the vision of the rule of God that informs Jesus' parables characterize the relationship between God and his people?

3. Remember our discussion of the problems with Matthew's allegory of salvation history in the Great Supper. Apply that discussion to the conclusion of Matthew's Wicked Tenants. Why would that conclusion be unacceptable?

4. Read the image of the Vineyard in Isaiah 5:1ff. How is that passage reflected in Jesus' parable? How is the conclusion of the parable different from that in Isaiah?

5. What would you have done if you had been the owner of the vineyard? Do you think your approach would have been a better one in the situation? Why?

6. Find a contemporary example of the situation presupposed by one of the parables studied in this chapter. How did the various parties act? If they acted differently from those in the parable, what would they have had to do to act like them? What do you think would have happened if they had?

Appendix

THE PARABLES

Why Speak in Parables? (Mk. 4:10–12)

[10]And when he was alone, those who were about him with the twelve asked him concerning the parables. [11]And he said to them, "To you has been given the secret of the kingdom of God, but for those outside everything is in parables; [12]so that they may indeed see but not perceive, and may indeed hear but not understand; lest they should turn again, and be forgiven."

The Treasure (Mt. 13:44)

[44]"The kingdom of heaven is like treasure hidden in a field, which a man found and covered up; then in his joy he goes and sells all that he has and buys that field.

The Pearl (Mt. 13:45ff.)

[45]"Again, the kingdom of heaven is like a merchant in search of fine pearls, [46]who, on finding one pearl of great value, went and sold all that he had and bought it.

The Lost Sheep (Mt. 18:12–14)

¹²What do you think? If a man has a hundred sheep, and one of them has gone astray, does he not leave the ninety-nine on the hills and go in search of the one that went astray? ¹³And if he finds it, truly, I say to you, he rejoices over it more than over the ninety-nine that never went astray. ¹⁴So it is not the will of my Father who is in heaven that one of these little ones should perish.

The Lost Coin (Lk. 15:8–10)

⁸"Or what woman, having ten silver coins, if she loses one coin, does not light a lamp and sweep the house and seek diligently until she finds it? ⁹And when she has found it, she calls together her friends and neighbors, saying, 'Rejoice with me, for I have found the coin which I had lost.' ¹⁰Just so, I tell you, there is joy before the angels of God over one sinner who repents."

The Lamp (Mk. 4:21)

²¹And he said to them, "Is a lamp brought in to be put under a bushel, or under a bed, and not on a stand?"

Garment and Wineskins (Mk. 2:21ff)

²¹"No one sews a piece of unshrunk cloth on an old garment; if he does, the patch tears away from it, the new from the old, and a worse tear is made. ²²And no one puts new wine into old wineskins; if he does, the wine will burst the skins, and the wine is lost, and so are the skins; but new wine is for fresh skins."

Salt (Mk 9:50)

⁵⁰"Salt is good; but if the salt has lost its saltness, how will you season it? Have salt in yourselves, and be at peace with one another."

Strong Man (Mk. 3:27)

²⁷But no one can enter a strong man's house and plunder his goods, unless he first binds the strong man; then indeed he may plunder his house.

Going before the Judge (Mt. 5:25ff)

[25]"Make friends quickly with your accuser, while you are going with him to court, lest your accuser hand you over to the judge, and the judge to the guard, and you be put in prison; [26]truly, I say to you, you will never get out till you have paid the last penny.

Unclean Spirit (Mt. 12:43–45)

[43]"When the unclean spirit has gone out of a man, he passes through waterless places seeking rest, but he finds none. [44] Then he says, 'I will return to my house from which I came.' And when he comes he finds it empty, swept, and put in order. [45]Then he goes and brings with him seven other spirits more evil than himself, and they enter and dwell there; and the last state of that man becomes worse than the first. So shall it be also with this evil generation."

Children in the Market (Mt. 11:16–19)

[16]"But to what shall I compare this generation? It is like children sitting in the market places and calling to their playmates,

[17]'We piped to you, and you did not dance;
we wailed, and you did not mourn.'

[18]For John came neither eating nor drinking, and they say, 'He has a demon'; [19]the Son of man came eating and drinking, and they say, 'Behold, a glutton and a drunkard, a friend of tax collectors and sinners!' Yet wisdom is justified by her deeds."

The Prodigal Son (Lk. 15:11–32)

[11]And he said, "There was a man who had two sons; [12]and the younger of them said to his father, 'Father, give me the share of property that falls to me.' And he divided his living between them. [13]Not many days later, the younger son gathered all he had and took his journey into a far country, and there he squandered his property in loose living. [14]And when he had spent everything, a great famine arose in that country, and he began to be in want. [15]So he went and joined himself to one of the citizens of that country, who sent him into his fields to feed swine. [16]And he would gladly have fed on the pods that the swine ate; and no

one gave him anything. [17]But when he came to himself he said, 'How many of my father's hired servants have bread enough and to spare, but I perish here with hunger! [18]I will arise and go to my father, and I will say to him, "Father, I have sinned against heaven and before you; [19]I am no longer worthy to be called your son; treat me as one of your hired servants."' [20]And he arose and came to his father. But while he was yet at a distance, his father saw him and had compassion, and ran and embraced him and kissed him. [21]And the son said to him, 'Father, I have sinned against heaven and before you; I am no longer worthy to be called your son.' [22]But the father said to his servants, 'Bring quickly the best robe, and put it on him; and put a ring on his hand, and shoes on his feet; [23]and bring the fatted calf and kill it, and let us eat and make merry; [24]for this my son was dead, and is alive again; he was lost, and is found.' And they began to make merry.

[25]"Now his elder son was in the field; and as he came and drew near to the house, he heard music and dancing. [26]And he called one of the servants and asked what this meant. [27]And he said to him, 'Your brother has come, and your father has killed the fatted calf, because he has received him safe and sound.' [28]But he was angry and refused to go in. His father came out and entreated him, [29]but he answered his father, 'Lo, these many years I have served you, and I never disobeyed your command; yet you never gave me a kid, that I might make merry with my friends. [30]But when this son of yours came, who has devoured your living with harlots, you killed for him the fatted calf!' [31]And he said to him, 'Son, you are always with me, and all that is mine is yours. [32]It was fitting to make merry and be glad, for this your brother was dead, and is alive; he was lost, and is found.'"

Man with Two Sons (Mt. 21:28–31a)

[28]"What do you think? A man had two sons; and he went to the first and said, 'Son, go and work in the vineyard today.' [29]And he answered, 'I will not'; but afterward he repented and went. [30]And he went to the second and said the same; and he answered, 'I go, sir,' but did not go. [31]Which of the two did the will of his father?" They said, "the first."

The Rich Man and Lazarus (Lk. 16:19–31)

[19]"There was a rich man, who was clothed in purple and fine linen and who feasted sumptuously every day. [20]And at his gate lay a poor man named Lazarus, full of sores, [21]who desired to be fed with what fell from the rich man's table; moreover the dogs came and licked his sores. [22]The poor man died and was carried by the angels to Abraham's bosom. The rich man also died and was buried; [23]and in Hades, being in torment, he lifted up his eyes, and saw Abraham far off and Lazarus in his bosom. [24]And he called out, 'Father Abraham, have mercy upon me, and send Lazarus to dip the end of his finger in water and cool my tongue; for I am in anguish in this flame.' [25]But Abraham said, 'Son, remember that you in your lifetime received your good things, and Lazarus in like manner evil things; but now he is comforted here, and you are in anguish. [26]And besides all this, between us and you a great chasm has been fixed, in order that those who would pass from here to you may not be able; and none may cross from there to us.' [27]And he said, 'Then I beg you, father, to send him to my father's house, [28]for I have five brothers, so that he may warn them, lest they also come into this place of torment.' [29]But Abraham said, 'They have Moses and the prophets; let them hear them.' [30]And he said, 'No, father Abraham; but if some one goes to him from the dead, they will repent.' [31]He said to him, 'If they do not hear Moses and the prophets, neither will they be convinced if some one should rise from the dead.' "

The Rich Fool (Lk. 12:16–21)

[16]And he told them a parable, saying, "The land of a rich man brought forth plentifully; [17]and he thought to himself, 'What shall I do, for I have nowhere to store my crops?' [18]And he said, 'I will do this: I will pull down my barns, and build larger ones; and there I will store all my grain and my goods. [19]And I will say to my soul, Soul, you have ample goods laid up for many years; take your ease, eat, drink, be merry.' [20]But God said to him, 'Fool! This night your soul is required of you; and the things you have prepared, whose will they be?' [21]So is he who lays up treasure for himself, and is not rich toward God."

The Sower (Mk. 4:3–8)

³"Listen! A sower went out to sow. ⁴And as he sowed, some seed fell along the path, and the birds came and devoured it. ⁵Other seed fell on rocky ground, where it had not much soil, and immediately it sprang up, since it had no depth of soil; ⁶and when the sun rose it was scorched, and since it had no root it withered away. ⁷Other seed fell among thorns and the thorns grew up and choked it, and it yielded no grain. ⁸And other seeds fell into good soil and brought forth grain, growing up and increasing and yielding thirtyfold and sixtyfold and a hundredfold."

Seed Growing Secretly (Mk. 4:26–29)

²⁶And he said, "The kingdom of God is as if a man should scatter seed upon the ground, ²⁷and should sleep and rise night and day, and the seed should sprout and grow, he knows not how. ²⁸The earth produces of itself, first the blade, then the ear, then the full grain in the ear. ²⁹But when the grain is ripe, at once he puts in the sickle, because the harvest has come."

Wheat and the Tares (Mt. 13:24–30)

²⁴Another parable he put before them, saying, "The kingdom of heaven may be compared to a man who sowed good seed in his field; ²⁵but while men were sleeping, his enemy came and sowed weeds among the wheat, and went away. ²⁶So when the plants came up and bore grain, then the weeds appeared also. ²⁷And the servants of the householder came and said to him, 'Sir, did you not sow good seed in your field? How than has it weeds?' ²⁸He said to them, 'An enemy has done this.' The servants said to him, 'Then do you want us to go and gather them?' ²⁹But he said, 'No; lest in gathering the weeds you root up the wheat along with them. ³⁰Let both grow together until the harvest; and at harvest time I will tell the reapers, Gather the weeds first and bind them in bundles to be burned, but gather the wheat into my barn.' "

Mustard Seed (Mk. 4:30–32)

³⁰And he said, "With what can we compare the kingdom of God, or what parable shall we use for it? ³¹It is like a grain of mustard seed, which, when sown upon the ground, is the smallest of all the seeds on earth; ³²yet when it is sown it grows up and becomes the greatest of all shrubs, and puts forth large branches, so that the birds of the air can make nests in its shade."

Leaven (Mt. 13:33)

³³He told them another parable. "The kingdom of heaven is like leaven which a woman took and hid in three measures of meal, till it was all leavened."

The Great Supper (Lk. 14:16–24)

¹⁶But he said to him, "A man once gave a great banquet, and invited many; ¹⁷and at the time for the banquet he sent his servant to say to those who had been invited, 'Come; for all is now ready.' ¹⁸But they all alike began to make excuses. The first said to him, 'I have bought a field, and I must go out and see it; I pray you, have me excused.' ¹⁹And another said, 'I have bought five yoke of oxen, and I go to examine them; I pray you, have me excused.' ²⁰And another said, 'I have married a wife, and therefore I cannot come.' ²¹So the servant came and reported this to his master. Then the householder in anger said to his servant, 'Go out quickly to the streets and lanes of the city, and bring in the poor and maimed and blind and lame.' ²²And the servant said, 'Sir, what you commanded has been done, and still there is room.' ²³And the master said to the servant, 'Go out to the highways and hedges, and compel people to come in, that my house may be filled. ²⁴For I tell you, none of those men who were invited shall taste my banquet.' "

Wedding Garment (Mt. 22:11–14)

¹¹"But when the king came in to look at the guests, he saw there a man who had no wedding garment; ¹²and he said to him,

'Friend, how did you get in here without a wedding garment?' And he was speechless. [13]Then the king said to the attendants, 'Bind him hand and foot, and cast him into the outer darkness; there men will weep and gnash their teeth.' [14]For many are called, but few are chosen."

Places at Table (Lk. 14:7–11)

[7]Now he told a parable to those who were invited, when he marked how they chose the places of honor, saying to them, [8]"When you are invited by any one to a marriage feast, do not sit down in a place of honor, lest a more eminent man than you be invited by him; [9]and he who invited you both will come and say to you, 'Give place to this man,' and then you will begin with shame to take the lowest place. [10]But when you are invited, go and sit in the lowest place, so that when your host comes he may say to you, 'Friend, go up higher'; then you will be honored in the presence of all who sit at table with you. [11]For every one who exalts himself will be humbled, and he who humbles himself will be exalted."

Shut Door (Lk. 13:24–30)

[24]"Strive to enter by the narrow door; for many, I tell you, will seek to enter and will not be able. [25]When once the householder has risen up and shut the door, you will begin to stand outside and to knock at the door, saying, 'Lord, open to us.' He will answer you, 'I do not know where you come from.' [26]Then you will begin to say, 'We ate and drank in your presence, and you taught in our streets.' [27]But he will say, 'I tell you, I do not know where you come from; depart from me, all you workers of iniquity!' [28]There you will weep and gnash your teeth, when you see Abraham and Isaac and Jacob and all the prophets in the kingdom of God and you yourselves thrust out. [29]And men will come from east and west, and from north and south, and sit at table in the kingdom of God. [30]And behold, some are last who will be first, and some are first who will be last."

Ten Virgins (Mt. 25:1–13)

[1]"Then the kingdom of heaven shall be compared to ten maidens who took their lamps and went to meet the bridegroom.

²Five of them were foolish, and five were wise. ³For when the foolish took their lamps, they took no oil with them; ⁴but the wise took flasks of oil with their lamps. ⁵As the bridegroom was delayed, they all slumbered and slept. ⁶But at midnight there was a cry, 'Behold, the bridegroom! Come out to meet him.' ⁷Then all those maidens rose and trimmed their lamps. ⁸And the foolish said to the wise, 'Give us some of your oil, for our lamps are going out.' ⁹But the wise replied, 'Perhaps there will not be enough for us and for you; go rather to the dealers and buy for yourselves.' ¹⁰And while they went to buy, the bridegroom came, and those who were ready went in with him to the marriage feast; and the door was shut. ¹¹Afterward the other maidens came also, saying, 'Lord, lord, open to us.' ¹²But he replied, 'Truly, I say to you, I do not know you.' ¹³Watch therefore, for you know neither the day nor the hour.''

The Good Samaritan (Lk. 10:29–37)

²⁹But he, desiring to justify himself, said to Jesus, "And who is my neighbor?" ³⁰Jesus replied, "A man was going down from Jerusalem to Jericho, and he fell among robbers, who stripped him and beat him, and departed, leaving him half dead. ³¹Now by chance a priest was going down that road; and when he saw him he passed by on the other side. ³²So likewise a Levite, when he came to the place and saw him, passed by on the other side. ³³But a Samaritan, as he journeyed, came to where he was; and when he saw him, he had compassion, ³⁴and went to him and bound up his wounds, pouring on oil and wine; then he set him on his own beast and brought him to an inn, and took care of him. ³⁵And the next day he took out two denarii and gave them to the innkeeper, saying, 'Take care of him; and whatever more you spend, I will repay you when I come back.' ³⁶Which of these three, do you think, proved neighbor to the man who fell among the robbers?" ³⁷He said, "The one who showed mercy on him." And Jesus said to him, "Go and do likewise."

Unmerciful Servant (Mt. 18:23–35)

²³"Therefore the kingdom of heaven may be compared to a king who wished to settle accounts with his servants. ²⁴When he

began the reckoning, one was brought to him who owed him ten thousand talents; [25]and as he could not pay, his lord ordered him to be sold, with his wife and children and all that he had, and payment to be made. [26]So the servant fell on his knees, imploring him, 'Lord, have patience with me, and I will pay you everything.' [27]And out of pity for him the lord of that servant released him and forgave him the debt. [28]But that same servant, as he went out, came upon one of his fellow servants who owed him a hundred denarii; and seizing him by the throat he said, 'Pay what you owe.' [29]So his fellow servant fell down and besought him, 'Have patience with me, and I will pay you.' [30]He refused and went and put him in prison till he should pay the debt. [31]When his fellow servants saw what had taken place, they were greatly distressed, and they went and reported to their lord all that had taken place. [32]Then his lord summoned him and said to him, 'You wicked servant! I forgave you all that debt because you besought me; [33]and should not you have had mercy on your fellow servant, as I had mercy on you?' [34]And in anger his lord delivered him to the jailers, till he should pay all his debt. [35]So also my heavenly Father will do to every one of you, if you do not forgive your brother from your heart."

Vineyard Workers (Mt. 20:1–16)

[1]"For the kingdom of heaven is like a householder who went out early in the morning to hire laborers for his vineyard. [2]After agreeing with the laborers for a denarius a day, he sent them into his vineyard. [3]And going out about the third hour he saw others standing idle in the market place; [4]and to them he said, 'You go into the vineyard too, and whatever is right I will give you.' So they went. [5]Going out again about the sixth hour and the ninth hour, he did the same. [6]And about the eleventh hour he went out and found others standing; and he said to them, 'Why do you stand here idle all day?' [7]They said to him, 'Because no one has hired us.' He said to them, 'You go into the vineyard too.' [8]And when evening came, the owner of the vineyard said to his steward, 'Call the laborers and pay them their wages, beginning with the last, up to the first.' [9]And when those hired about the eleventh hour came, each of them received a denarius. [10]Now when the first came, they thought they would receive more; but each of them also received a denarius. [11]And on receiving it they

grumbled at the householder, [12]saying, 'These last worked only one hour, and you have made them equal to us who have borne the burden of the day and the scorching heat.' [13]But he replied to one of them, 'Friend, I am doing you no wrong; did you not agree with me for a denarius? [14]Take what belongs to you, and go; I choose to give to this last as I give to you. [15]Am I not allowed to do what I choose with what belongs to me? Or do you begrudge my generosity?' [16]So the last will be first, and the first last."

The Talents (Mt. 25:14–30)

[14]"For it will be as when a man going on a journey called his servants and entrusted to them his property; [15]to one he gave five talents, to another two, to another one, to each according to his ability. Then he went away. [16]He who had received the five talents went at once and traded with them; and he made five talents more. [17]So also, he who had the two talents made two talents more. [18]But he who had received the one talent went and dug in the ground and hid his master's money. [19]Now after a long time the master of those servants came and settled accounts with them. [20]And he who had received the five talents came forward, bringing five talents more, saying, 'Master, you delivered to me five talents; here I have made five talents more.' [21]His master said to him, 'Well done, good and faithful servant; you have been faithful over a little, I will set you over much; enter into the joy of your master.' [22]And he also who had the two talents came forward, saying, 'Master, you delivered to me two talents; here I have made two talents more.' [23]His master said to him, 'Well done, good and faithful servant; you have been faithful over a little, I will set you over much; enter into the joy of your master.' [24]He also who had received the one talent came forward, saying, 'Master, I knew you to be a hard man, reaping where you did not sow, and gathering where you did not winnow; [25]so I was afraid, and I went and hid your talent in the ground. Here you have what is yours.' [26]But his master answered him, 'You wicked and slothful servant! You knew that I reap where I have not sowed, and gather where I have not winnowed? [27]Then you ought to have invested my money with the bankers, and at my coming I should have received what was my own with interest. [28]So take the talent from him, and give it to him who has the ten talents. [29]For to everyone who has will more be given, and

he will have abundance; but from him who has not, even what he has will be taken away. ³⁰And cast the worthless servant into the outer darkness; there men will weep and gnash their teeth.' "

Doorkeeper (Mk. 13:33–37)

³³"Take heed, watch; for you do not know when the time will come. ³⁴It is like a man going on a journey, when he leaves home and puts his servants in charge, each with his work, and commands the doorkeeper to be on the watch. ³⁵Watch therefore–for you do not know when the master of the house will come, in the evening, or at midnight, or at cockcrow, or in the morning–³⁶ lest he come suddenly and find you asleep. ³⁷And what I say to you I say to all: Watch."

Faithful Servant (Mt. 24:45–51)

⁴⁵"Who then is the faithful and wise servant, whom his master has set over his household, to give them their food at the proper time? ⁴⁶Blessed is that servant whom his master when he comes will find so doing. ⁴⁷Truly, I say to you, he will set him over all his possessions. ⁴⁸But if that wicked servant says to himself, 'My master is delayed,' ⁴⁹and begins to beat his fellow servants, and eats and drinks with the drunken, ⁵⁰the master of that servant will come on a day when he does not expect him and at an hour he does not know, ⁵¹and will punish him, and put him with the hypocrites; there men will weep and gnash their teeth."

The Sheep and the Goats (Mt. 25:31–46)

³¹"When the Son of man comes in his glory, and all the angels with him, then he will sit on his glorious throne. ³²Before him will be gathered all the nations, and he will separate them one from another as a shepherd separates the sheep from the goats, ³³and he will place the sheep at his right hand, but the goats at the left. ³⁴Then the King will say to those at his right hand, 'Come, O blessed of my Father, inherit the kingdom prepared for you from the foundation of the world; ³⁵for I was hungry and you gave me food, I was thirsty and you gave me drink, I was a stranger and you welcomed me, ³⁶I was naked and you clothed me, I was sick and you visited me, I was in prison and

you came to me.' [37]Then the righteous will answer him, 'Lord, when did we see thee hungry and feed thee, or thirsty and give thee drink? [38]And when did we see thee a stranger and welcome thee, or naked and clothe thee? [39]And when did we see thee sick or in prison and visit thee?' [40]And the King will answer them, 'Truly, I say to you, as you did it to one of the least of these my brethren, you did it to me.' [41]Then he will say to those at his left hand, 'Depart from me, you cursed, into the eternal fire prepared for the devil and his angels; [42]for I was hungry and you gave me no food, I was thirsty and you gave me no drink, [43]I was a stranger and you did not clothe me, sick and in prison and you did not visit me.' [44]Then they also will answer, 'Lord, when did we see thee hungry or thirsty or a stranger or naked or sick or in prison, and did not minister to thee?' [45]Then he will answer them, 'Truly, I say to you, as you did it not to one of the least of these, you did it not to me.' [46]And they will go away into eternal punishment, but the righteous into eternal life."

Unjust Steward (Lk. 16:1–8a)

[1]He also said to the disciples, "There was a rich man who had a steward, and charges were brought to him that this man was wasting his goods. [2]And he called him and said to him, 'What is this that I hear about you? Turn in the account of your stewardship, for you can no longer be steward.' [3]And the steward said to himself, 'What shall I do, since my master is taking the stewardship away from me? I am not strong enough to dig, and I am ashamed to beg. [4]I have decided what to do, so that people may receive me into their houses when I am put out of the stewardship.' [5]So, summoning his master's debtors one by one, he said to the first, 'How much do you owe my master?' [6]He said, 'A hundred measures of oil.' And he said to him, 'Take your bill, and sit down quickly and write fifty.' [7]Then he said to another, 'And how much do you owe?' He said, 'A hundred measures of wheat.' He said to him, 'Take your bill, and write eighty.' [8]The master commended the dishonest steward for his prudence."

The Pharisee and the Tax-Collector (Lk. 18:9–14)

[9]He also told this parable to some who trusted in themselves that they were righteous and despised others: [10]"Two men went

up into the temple to pray, one a Pharisee and the other a tax collector. ¹¹The Pharisee stood and prayed thus with himself, 'God, I thank thee that I am not like other men, extortioners, unjust, adulterers, or even like this tax collector. ¹²I fast twice a week, I give tithes of all that I get.' ¹³But the tax collector, standing far off, would not even lift up his eyes to heaven, but beat his breast, saying, 'God, be merciful to me a sinner!' ¹⁴I tell you, this man went down to his house justified rather than the other; for every one who exalts himself will be humbled, but he who humbles himself will be exalted."

Wicked Tenants (Mk. 12:1–11)

¹And he began to speak to them in parables. "A man planted a vineyard, and set a hedge around it, and dug a pit for the wine press, and built a tower, and let it out to tenants, and went into another country. ²When the time came, he sent a servant to the tenants, to get from them some of the fruit of the vineyard. ³And they took him and beat him, and sent him away empty-handed. ⁴Again he sent to them another servant, and they wounded him in the head, and treated him shamefully. ⁵And he sent another, and him they killed; and so with many others, some they beat and some they killed. ⁶He had still one other, a beloved son; finally he sent him to them, saying, 'They will respect my son.' ⁷But those tenants said to one another, 'This is the heir; come, let us kill him, and the inheritance will be ours.' ⁸And they took him and killed him, and cast him out of the vineyard. ⁹What will the owner of the vineyard do? He will come and destroy the tenants, and give the vineyard to others. ¹⁰Have you not read this scripture:

'The very stone which the builders rejected
    has become the head of the corner;
¹¹This was the Lord's doing,
    and it is marvelous in our eyes'?"

Help at Midnight (Lk. 11:5–8)

⁵And he said to them, "Which of you who has a friend will go to him at midnight and say to him, 'Friend, lend me three loaves; ⁶for a friend of mine has arrived on a journey, and I have nothing to set before him'; ⁷ and he will answer from within, 'Do

not bother me; the door is now shut, and my children are with me in bed: I cannot get up and give you anything"? [8]I tell you, though he will not get up and give him anything because he is his friend, yet because of his importunity he will rise and give him whatever he needs."

Unjust Judge (Lk. 18:1-8)

[1]And he told them a parable, to the effect that they ought always to pray and not lose heart. [2]He said, "In a certain city there was a judge who neither feared God nor regarded man; [3]and there was a widow in that city who kept coming to him and saying, 'Vindicate me against my adversary.' [4]For a while he refused; but afterward he said to himself, 'Though I neither fear God nor regard man, [5]yet because this widow bothers me, I will vindicate her, or she will wear me out by her continual coming.' " [6]And the Lord said, "Hear what the unrighteous judge says. [7]And will not God vindicate his elect, who cry to him day and night? Will he delay long over them? [8]I tell you, he will vindicate them speedily. Nevertheless, when the Son of man comes, will he find faith on earth?"

SELECTED BIBLIOGRAPHY

Ballard, P. H. 1972	"Reasons for Refusing the Great Supper." JTS 23:341–50.
Beardslee, W. 1978	"Parable, Proverb and Koan." *Semeia* 12:151–77.
Breech, E. 1978	"Kingdom of God and the Parables of Jesus." *Semeia* 12:15–40.
Brown, P. 1978	*The Making of Late Antiquity.* Harvard.
Carlston, C. 1975a	*The Parables of the Triple Tradition.* Philadelphia: Fortress.
1975b	"Reminiscence and Redaction in Luke 15:11–32." JBL 94:368–90.
1980	"Proverbs, Maxims and the Historical Jesus." JBL 99:87–105.
Crespy, G. 1974	"The Parable of the Good Samaritan: An Essay in Structural Research." *Semeia* 2:27–50.
Crossan, J. D. 1971	"The Parable of the Wicked Husbandmen." JBL 90:451–73.
1973a	*In Parables.* New York: Harper & Row.
1973b	"The Seed Parables of Jesus." JBL 92:244–66.
1974a	"The Servant Parables of Jesus." *Semeia* 1:17–62.
1974b	"The Good Samaritan: Toward a Generic Definition of Parable." *Semeia* 2:82–112.

1975	*The Dark Interval: Towards a Theology of Story.* Niles, Ill.: Argus.
1976	*Raid on the Articulate: Comic Eschatology in Jesus and Borges.* New York: Harper & Row.
1979	*Finding Is the First Act: Trove Folktales and Jesus' Treasure Parable.* Philadelphia: Fortress.
1980	*Cliffs of Fall: Paradox and Polyvalence in the Parables of Jesus.* New York: Seabury.
Culler, R. 1975	*Structuralist Poetics.* Ithaca: Cornell.
Derrett, J. D. M. 1967/1968	"Law in the New Testament: The Parable of the Prodigal Son." NTS 14:56–74.
1974	"Workers in the Vineyard: A Parable of Jesus." 25:60–91.
Dodd, C. H. 1961	*The Parables of the Kingdom.* New York: Scribner's.
Donfried, K. 1974	"The Allegory of the Ten Virgins (Mt 25:1–13) as a Summary of Matthean Theology." JBL 93:415–28.
Doty, W. 1971	"An Interpretation: Parable of the Weeds and the Wheat." Int 25:185–93.
Fitzmyer, J. 1964 (1974)	"The Story of the Dishonest Manager." TS 25:23–42; reprinted in *Essays on the Semitic Background of the New Testament.* Missoula: Scholar's Press, 161–84.
Freud, S. 1961 (1931)	*Civilization and Its Discontents.* New York: Norton.
Freyne, S. 1980	*Galilee: From Alexander the Great to Hadrian.* Wilmington, Del.: Michael Glazier/ Notre Dame: Notre Dame.
Fuller, R. 1978	"The Double Commandment of Love: A Test Case for the Criteria of Authenticity." *Essays on the Love Commandment.* Philadelphia: Fortress, 41–56.
Funk, R. 1966	*Language, Hermeneutic and Word of God.* New York: Harper & Row.
1974a	"Structure in the Narrative Parables of Jesus." *Semeia* 2:51–73.

1974b	"The Good Samaritan as Metaphor." *Semeia* 2:74–81.
1975	*Jesus as Precursor*. Philadelphia: Fortress.
Gouldner, M. D. 1968	"The Characteristics of the Parables in the Several Gospels." JTS 19:51–60.
Hammerton-Kelly, R. 1979	*God the Father: Theology and Patriarchy in the Teaching of Jesus*. Philadelphia: Fortress.
Huffmann, N. A. 1978	"Atypical Features in the Parables of Jesus." JBL 97:207–20.
Jeremias, J. 1963 (rev)	*The Parables of Jesus*. New York: Scribner's.
Johnson, L. T. 1977	*The Literary Function of Possessions in Luke-Acts*. Missoula: Scholar's Press.
Johnston, R. M. 1976	"The Study of Rabbinic Parables: Some Preliminary Observations." *Society of Biblical Literature 1976 Seminar Papers*. Missoula: Scholar's Press, 337–57.
Kermode, F. 1979	*The Genesis of Secrecy*. Cambridge: Harvard.
Kerr, W. 1967	*Tragedy and Comedy*. New York: Simon & Schuster.
Linnemann, E. 1966	*Jesus of the Parables*. New York: Harper & Row.
Lynch, W. 1965	*Images of Hope*. New York: New American Library.
McGaughy, L. C. 1975	"The Fear of Yahweh and the Mission of Judaism: A Post-Exilic Maxim and Its Early Christian Expansion in the Parable of the Talents." JBL 94:235–45.
Meier, J. 1979	*The Vision of Matthew*. New York: Paulist.
Metz, J. B. 1980	*Faith in History and Society*. New York: Seabury.
Meyer, B. F. 1979	*The Aims of Jesus*. London: SCM.
Moule, C. F. D. 1977	*The Origin of Christology*. London: Cambridge.
Nickelsburg, G. W. 1979	"Riches, the Rich and God's Judgment in 1 En. 92–105 and the Gospel According to Luke." NTS 25:324–44.

Perrin, N.
1967

Rediscovering the Teaching of Jesus. New York: Harper & Row.

1976

Jesus and the Language of the Kingdom. Philadelphia: Fortress.

Ricoeur, P.
1974

"Fatherhood: From Phantasm to Symbol." *The Conflict of Interpretations.* Evanston: Northwestern, 468–97.

1975

"Paul Ricoeur on Biblical Hermeneutics." *Semeia* 4.

Robinson, J. A. T.
1962

"The Parable of the Sheep and the Goats." *Twelve New Testament Studies.* SBT 34. London: SCM, 76–93.

Sanders, J. T.
1975

Ethics in the New Testament. Philadelphia: Fortress.

Schillebeeckx, E.
1979

Jesus: An Experiment in Christology. New York: Seabury.

Scholes, R.
1974

Structuralism in Literature. New Haven: Yale.

Schottroff, L.
1978

"Non-Violence and the Love of Enemies." *Essays on the Love Command.* Philadelphia: Fortress.

Schwartz, H.
1976

Imperial Messages: One Hundred Modern Parables. New York: Avon.

Scott, R. B. Y.
1971

The Way of Wisdom in the Old Testament. New York: Macmillan.

Shibayama, Z.
1974

Zen Comments on the Mumonkan. New York: Harper & Row.

Smith, C. W. F.
1975 (rev)

The Jesus of the Parables. Philadelphia: Pilgrim.

Stendahl, K.
1976

Paul among Jews and Gentiles. Philadelphia: Fortress.

Sulloway, F.
1980

Freud: Biologist of the Mind. New York: Basic.

TeSelle, S.
1975

Speaking in Parables. Philadelphia: Fortress.

Tolbert, M.
1975

"The Prodigal Son: An Essay in Literary Criticism from a Psychoanalytic Perspective." *Society of Biblical Literature 1975 Seminar Papers.* Vol. 2. Missoula: Scholar's Press, 207–18.

1979   *Perspectives on the Parables: An Approach to
                              Multiple Interpretation.* Philadelphia: For-
                              tress.

Turner, V.   *Dramas, Fields and Metaphors: Symbolic Ac-
1974   tion in Human Society.* Ithaca: Cornell.

Via, D. O.   *The Parables.* Philadelphia: Fortress.
1966

1975   "The Prodigal Son: A Jungian Reading." *So-
                              ciety of Biblical Literature 1975 Seminar Pa-
                              pers.* Missoula: Scholar's Press, 219–32.

Wilder, A.   *Early Christian Rhetoric.* Cambridge: Har-
1971 (rev)   vard.

1974   "The Parable of the Sower: Naivete and
                              Method in Interpretation." *Semeia* 2:134–51.

1976   *Theopoetic.* Philadelphia: Fortress.

Wittig, S.   "A Theory of Polyvalent Reading." *Society of
1975   Biblical Literature 1975 Seminar Papers.* Vol.
                              2. Missoula: Scholar's Press, 169–84.

MODERN AUTHORS INDEX

217

PARABLES INDEX

SUBJECT INDEX

SCRIPTURE INDEX

(See Parables Index for Parable Citations)

INDEX OF OTHER ANCIENT TEXTS